Derwin Gray's passion for Jesus and the
Full of vivid personal stories, real-life ch
and spiritual energy, this book cannot f
God and our desire to see people transfe

> N. T. WRIGHT, research professor emeritus of New Testament and
> early Christianity at St Mary's College in the University of St Andrews
> and senior research fellow at Wycliffe Hall, Oxford

In *Lit Up with Love: Becoming Good-News People to a Gospel-Starved World*, Derwin masterfully unpacks the why and how of evangelism. This book is for everyone who cringes at the thought of evangelism and wonders why anyone would do it. It's not offering the latest method or technique; instead we are presented with a compelling vision of the extraordinary privilege it is to join Jesus in his quest to seek and save the lost.

> CHRISTINE CAINE, cofounder of A21 and Propel Women

As followers of Jesus, we know that our only hope is in the power of the gospel. Despite that recognition, many Christians hesitate to share its transformative power. In Pastor Derwin Gray's book *Lit Up with Love: Becoming Good-News People to a Gospel-Starved World*, he equips believers to confidently spread Jesus' message and shine a bright light into a dark world. This is a must-read for anyone who needs a renewed sense of purpose for reaching people with the gospel.

> CRAIG GROESCHEL, pastor of Life.Church and *New York Times* bestselling author

We need this book right now. The church needs course correction, and my friend Derwin is pointing us in the right direction with this timely work. I am thankful he has never lost his zeal for the great commission.

> BRADY BOYD, senior pastor of New Life Church

None of us would have found life and freedom in Jesus if someone hadn't told us about him. We are each the beneficiary of another's love, courage, and willingness to share the Good News. And yet many of us still struggle to pay it forward. We don't know what to say, or we don't want to offend, so we withhold what was so graciously given to us. If that describes your relationship with evangelism and you want to change but don't know how, this book is for you. With passion, conviction, inspiration, and clarity, Derwin has written a primer for evangelism. If you are looking for a first step to learn how to share your faith, look no further!

SHARON HODDE MILLER, author of *The Cost of Control*

Warning: Read at your own risk—because *Lit Up with Love* will ignite a missional imagination for a gospel-starved world. I am so grateful Dr. Gray has created a resource that will equip church leaders and churches to light up the dark with the love of Jesus as we shine like stars in this world.

BRENT CROWE, vice president of Student Leadership University

If you are curious about how to live empowered by the Holy Spirit and love others into the Kingdom of God, then *Lit Up with Love* is your go-to resource. Loving people out of the overflow of God's grace in our lives should be our top priority. However, loving people and loving the hard to love might be our greatest challenge. Our cultural moment requires us to dig deep into our souls and discover how to love with God's kind of love. Don't just read this book— read it and pass it on to someone else!

DR. ED LOVE, executive director of church multiplication and discipleship for The Wesleyan Church

Lit Up with Love is the guide we need to help us graciously and effectively share God's love with people in our real lives. These pages are a gift. Dr. Derwin Gray is one of the most important voices in the global church today, and we are blessed to learn what God has revealed to him about sharing the hope of Jesus with the people right next to us.

DR. HOSANNA WONG, international speaker and bestselling author of *How (Not) to Save the World*

Derwin has been a friend and brother to me for over twenty-five years, and in that time I've watched him live out everything he writes about in these pages. *Lit Up with Love* is personal, theological, practical, and most importantly . . . *doable!* This is simple evangelism, rooted in our love for Jesus, that every Christian can begin practicing right now.

CLAYTON KING, pastor, evangelist, and author of *Reborn* and *Stronger*

Dr. Derwin Gray is my pastor. He is an older brother in the Lord, and his investment in my life has fundamentally shaped and reshaped my ministry. He is infectious about evangelism and a love for those far from God. His zeal has ignited mine in a way that permeates my preaching, leadership, and personal life. What he has written in *Lit Up with Love* feels to me like a culmination of many lessons I have learned from him, and I know they will change your life and ministry too.

LÉONCE B. CRUMP JR., pastor of United Church and author of *Renovate* and *The Resilience Factor*

This is a timely call for Christians to embody the transformative love of Jesus in a world desperate for hope and healing. Gray weaves together personal stories, biblical insights, and practical advice, inviting us to become everyday missionaries who bring light to every corner of our communities. This book is not just an exposition of the Good News; it is a practical guide that equips us to live as messengers. Read and shine!

GLENN PACKIAM, lead pastor of Rockharbor Church and author of *The Resilient Pastor* and *The Intentional Year*

Derwin Gray is a divinely appointed and anointed force of nature as a pastor, leader, theologian, author, and man of God. Twenty years ago I had the privilege of touring with him during our Dare 2 Share conference tours. As we traveled across America equipping tens of thousands of teenagers to live and share their faith, I witnessed him light up every room he was in with the love of Christ. He became the unofficial tour pastor because of his passion for Jesus and love for everyone he encountered. In his excellent book *Lit Up with Love*, Derwin unpacks the powerful biblical insights that he has been living out for decades. I have been deeply impacted by his writings, but also, more than anything else, his life. You will leave this book energized, convicted, and inspired to be lit up with the love of Christ everywhere you go and with everyone you meet.

> **GREG STIER,** founder/visionary of Dare 2 Share and author of *Radical like Jesus*

Lit Up with Love is a powerful call to live with purpose, on mission, and with a heart for the gospel. With wisdom rooted in Scripture and a contagious passion, Pastor Derwin guides us on a journey to embrace our God-given calling. Whether you're new to faith or a seasoned believer, this book will inspire you to live intentionally for Christ and impact the world around you. I highly recommend it!

> **JONATHAN POKLUDA,** lead pastor of Harris Creek Baptist Church, bestselling author, and host of *Becoming Something*

Lit Up with Love: Becoming Good-News People to a Gospel-Starved World is just the right book for our present time. In a world desperately seeking answers and solutions to their pain and sorrows, followers of Christ must be ready to embrace and walk alongside others with genuine love. This book serves as a vital reminder of what it means to embody the light and love of Jesus, addressing the world's profound needs, starting within our own communities and extending to everyone we encounter daily. I highly recommend it and pray that it will be the motivation that we need to stay "lit" for Jesus.

> **PASTOR JOHN K. JENKINS SR.,** senior pastor of First Baptist Church of Glenarden and president of Converge

DERWIN L. GRAY

LIT UP WITH LOVE

Becoming Good-News People to a Gospel-Starved World

A NavPress resource published in alliance
with Tyndale House Publishers

NavPress.com

Lit Up with Love: Becoming Good-News People to a Gospel-Starved World

Copyright © 2025 by Derwin Gray. All rights reserved.

A NavPress resource published in alliance with Tyndale House Publishers

NavPress and the NavPress logo are registered trademarks of NavPress, The Navigators, Colorado Springs, CO. *Tyndale* is a registered trademark of Tyndale House Ministries. Absence of ® in connection with marks of NavPress or other parties does not indicate an absence of registration of those marks.

The Team:
David Zimmerman, Publisher; Caitlyn Carlson, Senior Editor; Elizabeth Schroll, Copyeditor; Olivia Eldredge, Managing Editor; Sarah K. Johnson, Proofreading Coordinator

Cover illustration of flame icon copyright © Julia Hansen/Depositphotos. All rights reserved.

Cover design by Ron C. Kaufmann

Author photo by Alexander Acevedeo, copyright © 2020. All rights reserved.

Unless otherwise indicated, all Scripture quotations are taken from the *Holy Bible*, New Living Translation, copyright © 1996, 2004, 2015 by Tyndale House Foundation. Used by permission of Tyndale House Publishers, Carol Stream, Illinois 60188. All rights reserved. Scripture quotations marked CSB have been taken from the Christian Standard Bible,® copyright © 2017 by Holman Bible Publishers. Used by permission. Christian Standard Bible® and CSB® are federally registered trademarks of Holman Bible Publishers. Scripture quotations marked ESV are from The ESV® Bible (The Holy Bible, English Standard Version®), copyright © 2001 by Crossway, a publishing ministry of Good News Publishers. Used by permission. All rights reserved. Scripture quotations marked NIV are taken from the Holy Bible, *New International Version,*® *NIV.*® Copyright © 1973, 1978, 1984, 2011 by Biblica, Inc.® Used by permission. All rights reserved worldwide.

Published in association with The Bindery Agency, thebinderyagency.com

For more resources from this author, see derwinlgray.com.

Some of the anecdotal illustrations in this book are true to life and are included with the permission of the persons involved. All other illustrations are composites of real situations, and any resemblance to people living or dead is purely coincidental.

For information about special discounts for bulk purchases, please contact Tyndale House Publishers at csresponse@tyndale.com, or call 1-855-277-9400.

ISBN 978-1-64158-859-1

Printed in the United States of America

31	30	29	28	27	26	25
7	6	5	4	3	2	1

To Alan Bacon Sr. (1958–2023),

I am sad you aren't here to read my book. But I am also celebrating that you are with the One my book is about: King Jesus.

You were more than a friend and mentor—you were like a father. Late at night and early in the morning, you graciously answered what must have seemed like a hundred calls from me. As I watched you live out being a faithful husband and loving father, you were training me to be a husband and father. As you patiently answered my questions about the Bible, theology, the gospel, and doctrine, searing into me a love for Jesus and the Word of God, you were training me to be a pastor-theologian. I would not be a pastor or have my doctorate if not for you.

You loved seeing people come to know Jesus: as you served the homeless and shared the gospel with anyone who would listen; as you faithfully worked for the Indianapolis Department of Public Works for nearly thirty-five years; as you served as a chaplain for the Indianapolis Metropolitan Police Department for twenty-three years. Sitting at your feet, I learned how to be a disciple of King Jesus who loves his wife, his children, the church, and lost people. And my heart for evangelism was inspired by yours.

Mary, your teenage sweetheart and precious wife of forty-eight years, held you in her arms as you took your last breath on earth. And King Jesus held you in his arms when you took your first breath in eternity. I know you heard Jesus whisper, "Well done, my good and faithful servant!"

Alan, I love you. See you later.

Contents

Part Three: Lit Up with Love

Foreword

The church in the United States is hurting. So many of the people around us aren't interested in the Good News of Jesus because they're wary about, disinterested in, or opposed to what they see of Christianity. Even some of those who once sat beside us on Sundays no longer see what's compelling about this faith that is supposed to lead to the abundant life.

On top of this, there's a whole lot of criticism out there about the church. Our culture talks a lot about what Christians are doing wrong. And, as my friend Derwin Gray has identified, it's because we've forgotten what brought us to Jesus in the first place. When we remember our first love, when we experience and are motivated and energized by the love of God, we become people who want everyone else around us to experience that love too. We see their humanity, their dignity, their aches, their needs—and love moves us to meet them and to help them encounter the only Love who will satisfy.

Derwin's own journey—from being introduced to God while in the NFL to leading Transformation Church—is a powerful reminder of what happens when someone is lit up with the love of Jesus. From the first time he encountered Jesus' transformative love through a teammate, he became alive with this truth: Every believer is called and equipped to be an everyday missionary, sharing Christ's love in both ordinary and extraordinary ways. It doesn't have to be awkward or forced or impersonal. It's just love. Just seeing people God loves with the eyes and perspective of God and bringing God's love to their places of deepest hunger.

Derwin doesn't just talk about the core human longings for hope, rest, healing, and new life—he's lived them. And he's seen God meet these longings in other people and transform their lives again and again. That's why he's so passionate about helping the rest of us integrate the vision and discover the practical ways to live our faith with intention and love. His challenge to be "hope dealers" and "everyday missionaries" isn't just talk. He's a man of action. And he wants you to know you have everything you need to join Jesus in this mission to bring hope and love to people right where you are.

I care a lot about the church. I care a lot about Jesus' mission. I care a lot about everyday Christians getting up and doing something about a hurting world. *Lit Up with Love* is the call to action we need. May this book spark a fire in you to live boldly, love deeply, and be a Good-News person to those wandering in the dark.

Dave Ferguson
coauthor of *BLESS: 5 Everyday Ways to
Love Your Neighbor and Change the World*

WHERE ARE YOU GOING?

The End at the Beginning

I want to tell you about a new city.

This city is like no other, like nowhere you've ever been. Words like *war*, *poverty*, *racism*, *human trafficking*, *sexual immorality*, *greed*, and *unforgiveness* are not mentioned here. Evil does not exist. Sin, death, sorrow, and suffering are not even faint memories. All the world's sadness has become undone, remembered no more. The only tears in this city are tears of joy. Darkness cannot live here, for every corner of every street reflects a light source brighter than ten thousand suns, shining eternally, giving life.

This new city is completely lit up with love.

"I will create new heavens and a new earth;
the past events will not be remembered or come to mind.
Then be glad and rejoice forever
in what I am creating;
for I will create Jerusalem to be a joy
and its people to be a delight.
I will rejoice in Jerusalem
and be glad in my people.
The sound of weeping and crying
will no longer be heard in her."

ISAIAH 65:17-19, CSB

Your loved ones who died in the old city are alive in the new one. Your grandmother looks different, but she's still your granny. You feel every ounce of her love in a way you never did before. Your aunts and uncles and brothers and sisters and relatives from previous generations greet you. They are whole and beautiful; their "corruptible body is clothed with incorruptibility," and their "mortal body is clothed with immortality"[1]; they are now truly human, and it's glorious. They are alive.

Each one is lit up with love.

In this city of light, you also meet people you didn't know in the old city—but somehow you all know you are family. The blood of the One who lights up the city has made you a family, his family—a global, colorful, multiethnic village comprised of every nation, tribe, and tongue.[2] Everyone flourishes in this city. Their eyes reflect the joy of ultimate human flourishing.

Each inhabitant of the city is lit up with love.

All creation is more beautiful and more real than you imagined possible, just as it was intended to be from the beginning. The sky, trees, mountains, animals—all things are new and better and more magnificent than in the old city that passed away.

Every part of creation is lit up with love.

Just when you think the new city could not get any more splendid, you hear music and singing more wonderful than anything you've ever experienced. A holy symphony of praise surrounds you, harmonies woven in how people relate to each other and creation, thousands upon thousands of voices layering in one accord, in an eternal celebration. As you move closer to the singers, your eyes open wide, your heart beats fast. You are overwhelmed by the overflow of love and joy and laughter and tears and beauty and awe.

That's when you see him. Jesus, the glorious Lamb of God, the Light of the city and every person in it. And all you can do is join the multitude of people, lifting your voice in songs of praise.

You are worthy to take the scroll
and to open its seals,
because you were slaughtered,
and you purchased people
for God by your blood
from every tribe and language
and people and nation.
You made them a kingdom
and priests to our God,
and they will reign on the earth. . . .

Worthy is the Lamb who was slaughtered
to receive power and riches
and wisdom and strength
and honor and glory and blessing! . . .

Blessing and honor and glory and power
be to the one seated on the throne,
and to the Lamb, forever and ever!
REVELATION 5:9-10, 12-13, CSB

You are a blood-bought citizen of the new city, a royal priest, a coheir, ruling and reigning with the Lamb in the new heaven and new earth.[3] Every day is filled with worship, delight, fulfilling work, exploration of creation—and most of all, love.

Our destiny is set. Our eternal inheritance will be fulfilled. Our identity has been declared because we are united to Christ. And Love himself has called us home.

What would happen if our glorious future transformed how we work, love, suffer, and create in the present? We would be lit up with love, shining into the darkness. Our life and words would be good news.[4]

PART ONE

GOOD-NEWS PEOPLE

CHAPTER 1

LET'S TALK ABOUT GOOD NEWS

Participating in Restoration

Matt was an atheist. He wanted me to know that up front as we connected over a cup of coffee. He worked as a personal trainer, and one of his clients had shared her faith with him—but she didn't know where to start with answering his intellectual questions about evil and suffering. That's when she asked if he'd be open to meeting with me, and he agreed.

Matt and I talked primarily about the problem of evil and suffering, which seemed to be his main hang-up when considering Christ. I told him, "Being an atheist doesn't solve the problem of evil and suffering." Not believing in a higher power doesn't exempt you from experiencing evil or suffering. Christians suffer, too, but there's a key difference: We follow the Suffering Servant, who knows our pain and weaves redemptive purpose into our suffering.[1] On the cross Jesus experienced our suffering and our pain, and through his resurrection we also experience his resurrection power. Jesus said, "I have told you these things so that in me you may have peace. You will have suffering in this world. Be courageous! I have conquered the world."[2] Even when I don't understand or see his hand in the present moment, I trust Jesus to use my suffering and sorrow to form his character in me.[3] Jesus doesn't waste any of our pain—he recycles it into purpose. Suffering opens my eyes to the pain of others. It helps me understand the pain that Jesus endured on the cross. It gives me great hope knowing that one day suffering will be a thing of the past, but until that time, I am to experience the comforting presence of God in the crucible of suffering, and I am to be the comforting presence of God to those in pain.

I suggested to Matt that as an atheist, his very recognition that the world is unjust means there must be a standard of justice. And if there is a standard of justice, there must be someone who sets that standard: a God of justice. When we rail at the world for being wrong, we are longing for God to make it right.

I tried to help Matt see his questions as a key part of the Christian story: Sin, suffering, death, and evil are like a deadly virus that has infected every aspect of God's good creation. The darkness we see and experience was never meant to be, so God himself in the person of Jesus was sent on mission to rescue, redeem, restore, and reconcile humanity and creation through his life, death, and resurrection. God has already launched his work to make all things right—and through God's divine invitation, God's people get to participate in the restoration of creation.

New Testament scholar Michael J. Gorman puts it this way:

> God is on a mission to liberate humanity—and indeed the entire cosmos—from the powers of Sin and Death. . . . The fullness of this liberation is a future reality for which we may, and should, now confidently hope. It is nothing less than the prophetically promised new creation.[4]

The love that Matt needed to encounter was not only that Jesus' life, death, and resurrection forgives people of sins—but that God will heal all creation from the snare of evil and suffering.[5] Love equips us to see people's real needs and hear their honest pain. When we're lit up with God's love, we overflow with God's goodness in ways that answer the deepest questions of the people around us.

Lit Up with Love

Every single person hungers for divine love—even if they don't know it. They're looking for love at the bottom of a bottle they hope will finally numb the pain. They're seeking the Father's comfort when the latest hookup still doesn't silence the loneliness in their soul. They're longing for the Savior's tender validation of their worthiness even as they work themselves into a depressed, burned-out state. When the beauty of nature takes their breath away—and yet the awe is fleeting—they are yearning for the eternal Artist who created it. The Carpenter has crafted human beings with caring hands, and we can only be satified by him and his love.[6]

Our friends and our enemies—even people we have yet to meet—are looking for what we have: Jesus, the light and life of humanity. They just may not know it yet! That's where we come into play. We know this God who meets our deepest needs, forgives our worst sins, and turns our failures into triumphs.

So why is it so hard for us to share the healing work of Christ? Maybe we don't know where to start the conversation. Or perhaps we don't want to come across as arrogant (even though, ironically, our culture has never been louder about sharing what they believe).

This I know: The more we are lit up with love, the more we will share Christ. Those of us who know his love will not be able to contain it. We will burn brightly and catch others on fire.

The Jesus of Scripture, the God who is love,[7] was called a drunkard and a friend of sinners.[8] The sinners saw his holiness and felt the hope of a new life with him. We who were once sinners, now saints, now know the light of life. May we, too, become friends to sinners, inviting them to join us in the light.

Good News

As I see some people deconstructing their faith, others rejecting Jesus, and churches closing, I've sensed a burden from God—and that burden has become a calling. Some nights it's hard for me to sleep as I think about people who do not know Jesus and his life-transforming, soul-healing love.

How do we know God truly loves the world? Because God became flesh and walked among us, lived the life we never could live, died on the cross to forgive our sins, and rose from the dead to reconcile himself to us and to restore all creation. The world's true Lord, King Jesus, came to establish his rule and reign on the earth, conquering sin and death. His victory is absolute, and his followers share in his victory. A new day has dawned. A great light has overcome the darkness. And whoever comes to him in faith can participate in eternal life and in his rule and reign.[9]

I hunger to see more followers of Jesus become so overwhelmed by the beauty of salvation, so intoxicated by and immersed in God's deep love that they join him on his mission of reaching those dead in sin with his alive-making gospel of grace. I long for a movement of Good-News people so rooted in God's love that they can't help but share it with everyone they meet.

As we inhabit Christ and are lit up with his love, what does it look like to become Good-News people who sow gospel seeds into the hearts of other men and women?

- *When you're lit up with love, you know that only God saves. You reach out to others in love and confidence, recognizing that the results are up to him.* This is an incredibly freeing reality: As we join Jesus on his mission to reach lost people, he is the only One who saves. The triune God, the foundational missional community, allows us to participate in the process, but we are never responsible for the results. We don't have to use manipulation or gimmicks to save people. In Christ, we are free to love people and have gospel conversations, knowing that God is in charge of heart change. As speaker and teacher Ken Boa writes, "Divine sovereignty and human responsibility mysteriously mesh together in the evangelistic enterprise."[10] God is passionate about every human being having the opportunity to know him. He doesn't want "any to perish but all to come to repentance."[11] God wants people to experience salvation much more than we do.

- *When you're lit up with love, you embrace evangelism as a process, not a onetime event.* In John 4, Jesus uses agricultural imagery to teach his Jewish disciples about the process-oriented nature of evangelism. A farmer doesn't just show up and reap a harvest. She knows there's a process: preparing the soil, sowing seeds into it, and cultivating the soil so the seeds can flourish. Only after the Lord of creation brings life to the ground is there a harvest.

Generally, a person doesn't just come to faith in Jesus after one conversation. For each new believer, the Holy Spirit used

- someone to prepare the soil (that person's heart);
- someone to sow gospel seeds in the soil;
- someone to cultivate the soil; and
- someone who had the privilege of reaping the harvest.

No matter what part you play in this mysterious process, you are doing evangelism. We tend to make a big deal out of the harvesters, but the Holy Spirit empowers different people and different life circumstances to prepare one person's heart to receive the gospel invitation.[12] In God's story of redemption, each one of us plays a role in this beautiful mystery of the harvest.

- *When you're lit up with love, you see evangelism as an eternal investment.* In many ancient cultures, people were buried with their prized possessions in the hope that they could enjoy those treasures in the afterlife. Often, believers live as though we can take our homes, clothes, and money with us when we die. But we can only take the people we lead to Christ with us into the new heaven and new earth. The greatest investment we can make is sharing the gospel with people.

- *When you're lit up with love, you know that evangelism is holistic.* Jesus embodied and taught the gospel holistically. Through how he lived and what he preached, Jesus brought Good News that was healing balm to both the physical and the spiritual.[13] As followers of Jesus, we give hungry stomachs bread and hungry souls the Bread of Life.

- *When you're lit up with love, you know that evangelism and discipleship must be integrated.* Jesus commanded his followers to go and make disciples,[14] not just converts. A disciple is an apprentice of a master teacher. Jesus is the Master Teacher, and those of us who follow him are his apprentices. Disciples of Jesus choose to follow him, learning how to be citizens in the Kingdom of God through God's power. Jesus shares his life and power with his people so they can become living portraits of him.

That means we don't check a box off our to-do list and move on when someone makes a profession of faith. Our calling as Christians is to walk alongside others as they grow, helping them increasingly learn to live in the power of the Holy Spirit. As philosopher Dallas Willard writes,

> I am uncomfortable with the distinction between evangelism and discipleship. What we call evangelism is often nothing more than soul-winning. Evangelism has come to mean getting people "across the line." It operates according to a model of providing goods and services that has nothing to do with Christlikeness.
>
> The real question is, How do you do "evangelism-discipleship?" My short answer: You ravish people with the blessings of the Kingdom. You make them hungry for it. That's why words are so important—we must be wordsmiths. You use words to ravish people with the beauty of the kingdom. It's the beauty of the kingdom that Jesus said was causing people to climb over each other just to get in. People become excited like the pearl-purchaser—they will give everything to get in.[15]

Open your eyes. In the Spirit's power, help people comprehend the beauty of Jesus and his Kingdom. The harvest is all around you. See what Jesus sees, and bring others the love you have been given.

People of Light

About a year after that meeting with Matt, a church volunteer came to me just before the sermon and said that a man wanted to see me—and that he was crying uncontrollably.

It was Matt. His mother had just died. He fell into my arms. Tears soaked my shirt.

Matt and I met a few times after that. We grieved the death of his mother, read the Gospels, and talked about Jesus. Eventually, Matt became a follower of Jesus.

I asked him what moved him to follow Jesus. He talked about the despair of his wealthy clients, the hopelessness of his life, the wreckage of a failed marriage, his own patterns of sin he could not stop, and the death of his mother. And he talked about the love of God, how he now believed in the victory of Jesus over sin, death, and evil. Jesus' invitation to partner with him in healing the world moved Matt to give his life to Jesus. Matt was baptized. He joined our small group and continued his journey as a disciple of Jesus.

A simple conversation—where the love of God overflowed to meet Matt's deepest questions—sparked something in him that would take over a year to take root and grow. *When you're lit up with love, you understand that we are playing the long game.* It takes time for people to come to faith. Just because a person doesn't believe today doesn't mean they won't believe in the future.

In the pages of this book, we're going to walk together through the many ways the light and love of Jesus meet the world's deep need—and how we can participate in bringing that light to our communities and relationships. We're going to remember our first love and find that our fears around sharing our faith melt away when we focus on and immerse ourselves in Jesus. We will discover the multidimensional beauty of the gospel, learn to treasure Jesus above all, and learn how to become Good-News people to those around us.

My prayer is that after you read this book, you will love Jesus more than anything, be encouraged and equipped to speak and be the gospel to people who are longing to hear good news, and find yourself part of a growing community that becomes a movement of believers who are doing the same.

Friend, Jesus is worth it. We have the greatest treasure there is: Jesus.[16] May we share his goodness with the world.

Holy Habits

- *When you're lit up with love, you know that only God saves. You reach out to others in love and confidence, recognizing that the results are up to him.*

- *When you're lit up with love, you embrace evangelism as a process, not a onetime event.*

- *When you're lit up with love, you see evangelism as an eternal investment.*

- *When you're lit up with love, you know that evangelism is holistic.*

- *When you're lit up with love, you know that evangelism and discipleship must be integrated.*

- *When you're lit up with love, you understand that we are playing the long game.*

Reflection Questions

1. What are some of your deepest questions about life and the state of the world? How does the Good News of Jesus meet those?

2. How does the reality of salvation make you feel? How much are you aware of that reality in your everyday life?

3. Do you feel moved by what God has done for you? Why or why not? It's okay to be honest.

4. Why is understanding evangelism as a process important? How could this understanding create a movement of Good-News people all over the world?

5. What do you think it means to think of evangelism as holistic? Does that perspective change how you feel about evangelism?

PRAYER

Father,

Open my eyes to the light of Christ.

Holy Spirit,

Shine the light of Christ in me and through me

so the Father in heaven will be glorified.

King Jesus,

In a world of darkness, may my love shine, attracting people to you.

Give me the words to say.

In Jesus' name,

amen.

CHAPTER 2

WHAT IS THE GOOD NEWS?

Coming Alive in the Story of God

Whatever we love the most, we want others to experience and love too. I met my wife, Vicki, when I was eighteen and she was nineteen. We've now been married for thirty-three years. The older she gets, the more beautiful she becomes to me. There is no one on earth I love more. I've watched her walk through cancer, difficult pregnancies, and depression; serve our church courageously; do the hard work of allowing Jesus to heal her past hurts. And Vicki really loves me and our children. I have felt her love in how she has believed in me, respected me, and brought the best out of me. So when someone asks me about my wife, I'm excited and happy to tell people about her. Why? Because I love her. She's stunningly beautiful on the outside and inside.

As the love of Jesus permeates us and we taste his goodness, we hunger to share his redeeming love with lost people. The more we fall in love with Jesus, the more beautiful he becomes to us. *When you're lit up with love, you want others to experience Jesus' love and see his beauty.*[1]

Jesus is the star of the story of God, and we were created to live in that story. But often even those of us who follow Jesus do not know the full extent of God's story, the depth of how beautiful it is. And if we do not live in God's story, we will try to put God in our story. Instead of us worshiping God, God becomes a means to an end for our own glory. But seeking our own glory instead of God's is a death sentence from which we cannot save ourselves. When we share the gospel with those who don't know Jesus, we are partnering with Jesus to raise the dead, to free the captives, to open the eyes of the blind.[2] Salvation is inviting precious people to become alive, to step into the light and beauty of what they were created for: participating in God's redemptive drama of grace. *When you're lit up with love, you know the story of God, live in the story of God, and invite the lost into the story of God.*

Love at the Beginning

In a time before time, from eternity to eternity, there existed only the Light Bringer. All stories have an origin story except his. The Light Bringer is the origin of every other story.

This Light Bringer lives in an eternal community of love, unity, and beauty.[3] Nonmaterial, infinite, eternal, powerful beyond imagination, he holds time in his hand: All events—past, present, and future—are known to him. He has seen everything in one eternal glance. Everything the triune community of unity and beauty does follows from his sovereign love.

And out of that love, the Light Bringer decided to create something beautiful, a place where his boundless love could overflow. He spoke light into darkness. He spoke creation into being. Nothing became something, and that something was beautiful, good. Guided by life-giving love, the Light Bringer then moved to create the crown jewel of his creation: a man and a woman.

At that moment, creation became *very good*.

Of all creation, only the man and woman reflected the Light Bringer's likeness. These creatures of flesh, blood, bone, and guts bore the divine image, the creative impulse of their Maker.

Despite his transcendence, the Light Bringer desires to be in relationship with and live among his image bearers. He steps into his own creation. He dances and plays and loves and laughs with those he made. He invites them to *participate* in his life, his love, and his purpose for creation.

The image bearers are royal priests, *light bringers* in training. And the Light Bringer gives them a sacred task: to multiply and spread his glory on earth.

Darkness Descends

The image bearers had everything their hearts could desire. The Light Bringer was their source of life, the definer and designer of their identity, the giver of purpose. He created them to cocreate with him, to partner with him, relying on him to supply the light of life. But if they tried to create their own light, all the beauty would fade. Darkness and death would rush into the story.

And that is what happened. The man and woman listened to lies, following the voice of a creature who wanted to be the creator. "You can be in charge," the deceiver told them. "You can bring your own light." And so they tried to create their own light. Instead of believing the Light Bringer, the bearers of the divine image believed the deceiver.

Immediately beauty faded and darkness invaded. Shadows fell over the light of love, death grew like mold, and decay found its way into everyone and everything. Creation itself began to cry out in excruciating pain. From then on, every child born was infected with an incurable disease.

The Light Bringer wept.

But he had a plan. The darkness would not last—because the Light Bringer would not allow it.[4]

Light Breaks Through

Darkness mars and hides beauty. So the Light Bringer sent his light. Over and over, through centuries, ambassadors lit up with his love reminded the sons and daughters of the first man and woman of the beauty they were made for: love, not hate; mercy, not vengeance; generosity, not greed; truth, not lies.

The ambassadors carried the Light Bringer's portraits of grace, mercy, and kindness, showing the image bearers how beautiful the Light Bringer is and how beautiful creation could be again. But the image bearers rejected the messengers every time.

That's when the Light Bringer did something radical to rescue and restore his creation: In the mystery of the eternal community—the Father, the Son, and the Holy Spirit—the Son stepped out of eternity and into time to heal all creation. The Son lived and breathed and took on flesh among his creation, inviting those he loved to dance and play and love and laugh with him once again. The Son is the radiance of the Light Bringer's glory and "exact expression of his nature."[5] And the Son became the bridge to bring the Light Bringer and his art together again.[6]

The Son was lit up with love like no one had ever seen. He forgave the worst of sinners. He cared for the poor, the rich, the sick, the wicked, the religious, the pagan, the doubters, and the spiritual seekers. He said and lived beautiful things, like *Love and bless your enemies*; *If your enemy is hungry, feed him*; and *If they are thirsty, give them water.*[7] He proclaimed that he was the Way, the Truth, and the Life and that no one could get to the Light Bringer except through him.[8] He even dared to tell them that he was the Light Bringer.[9]

But the darkness fought back. Darkness did its best to destroy the light. And for a moment it seemed as though darkness had won.

But the darkness did not know that nothing could overcome the light.[10] The darker the times, the greater the light shines.[11] In his death, the Son took upon himself every piece of darkness that had invaded the image bearers. Darkness shut him in a tomb devoid of light, not knowing that light would roll the stone away. The Son rose from the dead. Light ascended.[12] The Light Bringer called his creation to come home to love, to come home to grace, to come and be beautiful again. And all those who heard his call to return home came and found that the love caught fire within them. They became light bearers to the world.

The Story of God

Living as Good-News people lit up with love isn't something we can do ourselves; we can do it only through the life of Christ residing within us. Through the indwelling presence and goodness of God the Holy Spirit, we're lit from the inside out when we walk by faith and embrace God's eternal love story,

- beginning with God the Father, God the Son, and God the Holy Spirit—YHWH—making human beings in his image, not because he needed us but because he wanted the abundance of his love to overflow;

- continuing when God didn't give up on his people even after they turned their backs on his abundant love and darkness entered the world;

- communicated through the life of Abraham, whom God called to father a multiethnic, global family;

- continued from Abraham through Isaac, Jacob, and the nation of Israel, a people meant to pick up the mantle dropped by Adam and Eve, to be light bringers, to become God's missionary force . . . who often failed;[13] and

- brought to fulfillment when God lit up the world with sacrificial, life-giving, sin-forgiving, death-defeating, evil-conquering love through the life, death, resurrection, and ascension of Jesus Christ.

Now God has a family who was purchased by Jesus. The new people of God join Jesus on his mission to bring more sons and daughters into his Father's family as they journey to the new promised land, the new heaven and new earth.

God has not only written the greatest love story ever—he has lived it! All Scripture points to Jesus, the hero of God's love story.[14] The better we know God's love story, the more it lights us up with love. The Hebrew Scriptures foretold that Jesus, the seed of Abraham, would give God a redeemed, colorful family.[15] I fear that all too often followers of Jesus are not lit up with love because they have a shallow understanding of God's story and the epic things he accomplished through Jesus. Jesus is not a sidebar to our faith; he is our faith![16]

Who Is Jesus?

When you're lit up with love, you know that Jesus is the eternal Son of God, Israel's Messiah, the world's true Lord and Savior, fully God and fully man. As the eternal Son of God, Jesus is united with God the Father. And because Jesus is also fully human, he is also united with—and representative of—humanity. Jesus alone reconciles God and humans through his sacrifice on the cross.[17] He is the sacred bridge of grace that humanity walks across into the Kingdom of God. How wonderful this is: The Son of God became human so humans can become sons of God,[18] sharing in the life of Christ.[19]

Why Was Jesus Sent?

When you're lit up with love, you know why Jesus was sent: to announce that the Kingdom of God was at hand and to proclaim the gospel.[20] Like a rudder helps steer a ship, knowing why Jesus came to earth leads you to worship him, commit to spiritual formation, and live on mission with him. Embracing Jesus as King means embracing his mission. As a member of the body of Christ, you are his hands and feet of service and his mouthpiece of grace. One of the ways Jesus moves on earth is through you. Just as his Father sent Jesus into the world, he now sends you.[21]

What Is the Kingdom of God?

When you're lit up with love, you know that the Kingdom of God is the rule and reign of God, embodied in the person of Jesus.[22] *King Jesus entered time and space to show us the Kingdom and invite us to participate in it.* Knowing that you are in Christ, that you are a royal priest, and that you share in the divine life of Jesus, you are empowered by the Spirit to reflect Jesus to the world. His life, his mission, his Kingdom are your foci now. As a citizen of God's Kingdom, you get to join Jesus in inviting people into the Kingdom of God.

Who Are the People of the Kingdom of God?

When you're lit up with love, you know that anyone who calls on the name of Jesus is reborn and transferred into God's Kingdom. From the beginning, God created his people to be a kingdom of priests, ministering grace, kindness, and love to others. Your life of love becomes a praise song for all the world to hear.[23] When you know that you are God's special possession, you want others to experience life in his Kingdom. He's too good to keep to yourself!

What Is Our Mission in the Kingdom of God?

When you're lit up with love, you are united with Christ and join him in his mission of reconciling the world to himself. Kingdom people are great-commandment and great-commission people, empowered by the great grace of God.[24] Knowing this is like having an internal compass that guides you on the path of life and helps you lead others toward that path.

What Is Our Destiny in God's Kingdom?

One day the Beautiful One, King Jesus, will return to judge the living and the dead, separate the sheep from the goats, and establish the new heaven and new earth for those who trust him. Those who chose to reject him, despite his sacrifice for them, will be eternally separated from him.[25] At last,

> God's dwelling [will be] with humanity, and he will live with them. They will be his peoples, and God himself will be with them and will be their God. He will wipe away every tear from their eyes. Death will be no more; grief, crying, and pain will be no more, because the previous things have passed away.
> REVELATION 21:3-4, CSB

When you're lit up with love, you know that those who belong to Christ will be raised from death and enjoy eternity in the new heaven and new earth—and that those who reject God's forgiving grace in the form of Christ will be eternally separated from him.[26] When we know this truth, a sense of urgency fuels us not only to love Jesus but also to make the love of Jesus known. Like the apostle Paul, we count all things as a loss compared to knowing Jesus![27]

The story of God is one of creation, fall, redemption, and consummation. The star of the story is Jesus. Anyone who calls upon the name of Jesus will pass from death to life, from judgment to acceptance, from orphan to child of the King. They become members of a new kind of community called the church, the bride of Christ. This new, multiethnic family is united to Jesus, is indwelt by the Holy Spirit, is formed into the image of Christ—and is his missionary team.

In 1925, missionary and theologian E. Stanley Jones wrote these words: "I saw that the gospel lies in the person of Jesus, that he himself is the Good News, that my one task was to live and to present him."[28] The joyous task of shining the light simply means telling others: "God loves you. Turn to him and be saved. Jesus is the best good news. He is worth sharing with the world."[29]

Holy Habits

- *When you're lit up with love, you want others to experience Jesus' love and see his beauty.*

- *When you're lit up with love, you know the story of God, live in the story of God, and invite the lost into the story of God.*

- *When you're lit up with love, you know that Jesus is the eternal Son of God, Israel's Messiah, the world's true Lord and Savior, fully God and fully man.*

- *When you're lit up with love, you know why Jesus was sent: to announce that the Kingdom of God was at hand and to proclaim the gospel.*

- *When you're lit up with love, you know that the Kingdom of God is the rule and reign of God, embodied in the person of Jesus. King Jesus entered time and space to show us the Kingdom and invite us to participate in it.*

- *When you're lit up with love, you know that anyone who calls on the name of Jesus is reborn and transferred into God's Kingdom.*

- *When you're lit up with love, you are united with Christ and join him in his mission of reconciling the world to himself.*

- *When you're lit up with love, you know that those who belong to Christ will be raised from death and enjoy eternity in the new heaven and new earth—and that those who reject God's forgiving grace in the form of Christ will be eternally separated from him.*

Reflection Questions

1. Do you tend to live in God's story or put God in your story? Why do you think that is?

2. What is beautiful to you about the story of God? What aspects of what you read are less familiar to you?

3. How would you explain the story of God to someone who doesn't know him?

4. How do you think remembering and going over the story of God daily would shift how you understand and experience his love?

5. What part of the Good News impacted you the most in this chapter? Why?

PRAYER

Father,

Teach me your story;

I want to live for your glory.

King Jesus,

Display your grace

so I can know my place in your story.

Holy Spirit,

Open the eyes of my heart

that I may see and seek the lost

so they may embrace grace and find their place in your story.

Amen.

PART TWO

A GOSPEL-STARVED WORLD

CHAPTER 3

STARVED FOR HOPE

Becoming Hope Dealers

I was in my midforties, seasoned by life, when I felt that my heart could finally handle looking back into my childhood. As I allowed God to give me the spiritual eyes to see, I could notice good. And I could look at the bad: the unspeakable trauma. At thirteen years old I was starving for hope, but I didn't know it. I wanted to run from the trauma I endured. I wanted to run from the toxic generational elements in my family. I wanted something better than what was around me.

Football was my way out. In high school, I was blessed with Christian coaches who offered structure and taught me discipline and grit. They told me that I was responsible for my own life! And that I could go to college!

Coach Rutledge and Coach Sullivan gave me hope that I could escape to something better. But the hope they gave me had a little *h*. It was hope I could create, hope I could manufacture myself. Eventually, that kind of hope runs out. For me, that little-*h* hope lost its power when I graduated from college and began my professional football career in 1993.

What I was really starving for was Hope with a big *H*. Hope that lasts. That Hope has a name: Jesus.

Jesus is the Hope who heals your trauma.
Jesus is the Hope who gives you a better future.
Jesus is the Hope who makes you a peacemaker in this violent world.

In our world, where pain and trauma and disaster and evil are in and around so much of our lives, hope can feel hard—even costly. But all human beings hunger for hope that lasts. As J. R. R. Tolkien wrote in the The Lord of the Rings, "Where there's life there's hope."[1] We have been given Hope that transfers us from death to true life. That's the Hope every single person needs.

Enemies of Hope

People who are lost in darkness attach their hopes to all sorts of created things: people, power, possessions. But the created things we place our hope in were never meant to save us but to point us to the Savior; they were never meant to satisfy us but to point us to the source of ultimate satisfaction; they were never meant to give us purpose but to be the arena in which God's purpose for our lives is placed on display.

There's a reason that happens. Christian theology teaches that there are three enemies of hope: the world, the flesh, and the devil.[2] These three enemies of hope point us to false sources of hope, deceiving us into believing that money, sex, and power can fix the deepest part of us that is broken. But not only do those things not sustain hope—they deform our lives, taking us down the path of destruction.

- **Money:** Poverty is a deep hole many people are trapped in. Financial stress, even when we are doing well by all worldly measures, can make us despair. A lack of money can seem to be the root of a lot of hopelessness, so having *more* money often seems like the antidote, the solution that will make us feel safe and secure for the long haul.

  I grew up on government assistance, and both my family and American culture told me that if I made enough money I would be happy. When my professional football career allowed me to buy name-brand clothes and vacations on tropical beaches, I thought I'd made it. When I was able to send money home to family back in Texas, I thought my money would fix the brokenness and heal the generational wounds. But I was still traumatized, insecure, and morally fractured. Money can't buy happiness. Money can't heal trauma or generational pain. Money can't forgive sins or make you stop sinning.

- **Sex**: An unhealthy understanding of sex is everywhere in our world, including the church, and it negatively affects our souls and relationships. For those who follow Jesus, sex between a husband and wife in the covenant of marriage is a sacred act of worship: the two becoming one, exploring the beauty of oneness and intimacy—emotionally, spiritually, and physically.[3] When this precious gift is misused, instead of oneness and intimacy, the sin of sexual immorality creates separation from the source of fulfillment, God. Instead of finding hope and happiness, we are left unfulfilled, with dysfunctional and disordered desires. But ultimately, our dysfunctional sexuality just leads to broken hearts and guilty souls.

  Sadly, I was exposed to sex in an unhealthy way at an early age. The sex talk I got at fourteen years old was "Don't get anyone pregnant." Watching porn in high school was as normal as doing homework. It wasn't until I met Jesus that I discovered that physical intimacy between a husband and wife could be an act of worship.

  Instead of sex becoming another unhealthy pursuit of hope for a happier life, in gospel living it can become what it was intended to be: a sacred act of worship within the covenant of marriage.

- **Power**: Often we equate feeling hopeful with feeling in control of our lives. If we think we're generally in charge of our own destinies—whether through how hard we work or who we know or the gifts and influence we have—we feel more secure. The more secure we feel, the more hope we have. And like a hamster on a wheel, we fight for control through wielding our power, thinking it will give us control so we can feel more secure, leading to hope. The logic of this massive lie is crushed under the weight of living in a fallen world. A cancer diagnosis shows we are not that powerful. Getting passed up for a promotion at work shows us we are not in control. Our spouse saying "I no longer love you; I want a divorce" shows us just how fragile life can be. Hope can be found in power. But it's not our power—it's God's: "May the God of hope fill you with all joy and peace as you believe so that you may overflow with hope by the power of the Holy Spirit."[4]

  When you grow up in a chaotic, out-of-control family environment like I did, you build your adult life around attempts to control everything, to minimize unpredictability and pain. But by my midtwenties I had learned I still had no control. I couldn't control whether my family would change. I couldn't control the injuries I suffered in football. I couldn't control what the future held. The more I sought power, the more the illusion of control slipped through my fingers. Living that lie is soul shattering—and hope shattering.

Before I met Jesus, I built my life on the shifting sands of money, sex, and power. Eventually storm clouds surrounded me, thunder roared, lightning flashed, monsoonal rain came, and my house of false hope was washed away.[5]

But now I see that storm as the floodwater of grace. Without false hope to hold me up, I hit rock bottom—and discovered that Jesus the Rock was there to catch me. I now stand on the Rock of Ages, in his "living hope."[6] Living Hope is a person who invites you to share in his life, mission, and eternal inheritance. This Hope is beautiful—and it lasts. I can hardly take it in!

People, power, and possessions can't stop the ache for hope. Only Hope himself can.

Hope Dealers

I started this book walking the streets of a new city where everything and everyone is lit up with love because of the One who is Love. That future with Jesus is the only source of true, sustaining hope. A vision of the future has the power to transform what you do today. This kind of hope involves the belief that a better tomorrow is coming and that it cannot be overcome by today's sin, sorrow, and suffering. *When you're lit up with love, you know that hope is found in the achievements of Jesus: in his sinless life; his substitutionary, atoning death; and his resurrection.*

Growing up where I grew up, I saw drug dealers on the street corners "slanging dope"—selling the devastation and death of addiction. But those of us who follow Christ are carrying the opposite: the life and hope of Jesus Christ, the ultimate Good News. What if every follower of Jesus got on their street corner and started slanging hope?

I often share with our Transformation Church congregation, "Get to your block and slang hope. In Christ, we are hope dealers! Hope has a name, and his name is Jesus."

When you're lit up with love, you accept Jesus' invitation to become a hope dealer.

Your sphere of influence is your block.

Your job.

Your school.

Your neighborhood.

Your CrossFit group.

Hope dealers delight in Jesus, adore him, and by faith experience his hope-transforming love. Hope dealers are men and women of prayer who have unshakable confidence in the saving grace of Jesus and who intentionally live their lives on mission with Jesus, looking for the lost.

- Hope dealers start their day praying, *Father, bring lost people my way.*
- Hope dealers understand and look for ways to live out their purpose: to know Jesus and make him known.
- Hope dealers trust the power of the Holy Spirit to grow the gospel seeds planted in the soil of people's hearts.

When you're lit up with love, you are a hope dealer to everyone you encounter. As I sat at a coffee shop working on this chapter, I noticed a woman with a German accent and a man with a Greek accent at the table next to me. I mentioned that I had just returned from Germany and that I love Greece. When they asked what I do professionally, I told them that I am a pastor and a New Testament scholar. They were interested in my story, so I shared the gospel with them in a natural, inviting way. Before they left, they asked if they could attend our Christmas Eve services, and I gave them a card that would lead them to our church website, my testimony, and my sermons.

Being a hope dealer is as simple as that. *When you're lit up with love, you know that no one person brings someone to Jesus.* Hope dealers cast seeds of grace and trust the Holy Spirit, who causes the seeds to take root and grow.[7]

Every day, wake up, get to your block, and slang hope.

Holy Habits

- *When you're lit up with love, you know that hope is found in the achievements of Jesus: in his sinless life; his substitutionary, atoning death; and his resurrection.*

- *When you're lit up with love, you accept Jesus' invitation to become a hope dealer.*

- *When you're lit up with love, you are a hope dealer to everyone you encounter.*

- *When you're lit up with love, you know that no one person brings someone to Jesus.*

Reflection Questions

1. What are some little-*h* hopes you turn to for security or comfort? How are those different from the Hope that lasts?

2. Identify someone in your life who needs hope. How could the hope of Christ help them out of their hopelessness?

3. Reflect on the Christian vision of future hope. How does focusing on that future change your perspective today? How could that vision of hope help you reach people?

4. What is your block—your sphere of influence?

5. What are some specific ways you can be a hope dealer today?

PRAYER

Holy Spirit,

In a world of hopelessness, may the blessed Hope, King Jesus,

be the delight and light of my life.

Bring lost people across my path so I can show them Jesus.

King Jesus,

You entered our dark world to show us the light.

In your life, death, and resurrection,

you accomplished the victory for humanity,

freeing us from sin, death, and the dark powers.

With eternal gratitude, I say thank you!

Father,

Thank you that in Jesus, I have the forgiveness of sins, resurrection power,

and future glory that give me power to live today.

Show me my block so I can slang hope!

Amen.

CHAPTER 4

STARVED FOR REST

Offering the Good Shepherd's Comfort

On a trip to Israel, I saw something I'll never forget: two kids, a boy of probably twelve and a girl who was maybe seven, shepherding a flock of sheep on a hillside. The girl was wearing a pink sweater with the word **LOVE** in big, bold letters across the front. I stepped closer to take a picture, and before I knew it, I was surrounded by sheep.

I know next to nothing about shepherding sheep. But I have enough sense to imagine what a good shepherd does: guide the sheep to a place of sustenance and safety, one full of green grass and plenty of water that offers rest from potential attacks from wolves.

In our modern world, soul fatigue is rampant. People are weary from their endless attempts to impress other people, who themselves are too tired to notice. People are exhausted from the futile effort of living a double life—curating a perfect "my best life now" image on social media while finding themselves living in an unfulfilled reality. Worse, people are depleted from the vicious cycle of trying to save themselves from destructive patterns of behavior.

Teenagers are tired.

College students are tired.

Young adults are tired.

Middle-aged people are tired.

Older people are tired.

Everybody's tired.

People think, *My job will give me green pastures.* It will not.

People believe, *My money will give me quiet waters.* It will not.

People are tired because wolves are relentlessly chasing them: toxic behaviors that poison their relationships; comparison that steals their joy; fear of an uncertain future, which increases their anxiety; and untended pain that reinjures their souls.

Like sheep, people need guidance and protection.

Like sheep, people need nourishment and rest.

Like sheep, people need a loving shepherd.

No matter how hard we try to protect ourselves from circling wolves and find our own rest, we cannot make green pastures or quiet waters. But *when you're lit up with love, you can introduce tired, lost sheep to the Good Shepherd, who can bring them to a place of refreshment and restoration.*[1]

The Good Shepherd

In the dusty hills of Israel, David, a shepherd boy who became king of Israel, wrote,

> The LORD is my shepherd, I lack nothing.
>> He makes me lie down in green pastures,
> he leads me beside quiet waters,
>> he refreshes my soul.
> He guides me along the right paths
>> for his name's sake.
> Even though I walk
>> through the darkest valley,
> I will fear no evil,
>> for you are with me;
> your rod and your staff,
>> they comfort me.

You prepare a table before me
>in the presence of my enemies.
You anoint my head with oil;
>my cup overflows.
Surely your goodness and love will
>follow me
>all the days of my life,
and I will dwell in the house of
>the LORD
>forever.

PSALM 23:1-6, NIV

David wrote about YHWH, the Shepherd-God of Israel. God as shepherd is a metaphor used again and again throughout Scripture to describe God's relationship with his people, but what God inspired David to write in Psalm 23 reveals how these Old Testament names for YHWH are part of this Lord who is our Shepherd:

PSALM 23	NAME FOR GOD[2]	MEANING
"The LORD is my shepherd"	Jehovah-Raah	The LORD our shepherd
"I lack nothing"	Jehovah-Jireh	The LORD will provide
"He refreshes my soul"	Jehovah-Rapha	The LORD will heal (or restore)
"He guides me along the right paths"	Jehovah-Tsidkenu	The LORD our righteousness
"For you are with me"	Jehovah-Shammah	The LORD is there
"Your rod and your staff, they comfort me"	Jehovah-Shalom	The LORD our peace
"You prepare a table before me in the presence of my enemies"	Jehovah-Nissi	The LORD our banner

YHWH the Shepherd is attentive to his people, near his people, caring for his people, leading his people, protecting his people, providing for his people, nourishing his people. *When you're lit up with love, you live in the confidence that Jesus, the Good Shepherd, is all that his sheep need.* We have an all-sufficient Savior who wants us to know him and follow his voice.

When my children were babies, they knew their mama. For nine months, Presley and Jeremiah experienced life in their mother's womb; her life provided them with life. They recognized Vicki's gentle whisper. They knew she was their source of nourishment. They knew to turn to her because they had experienced their mother's love and protection.

Like babies held in their mothers' arms, Jesus' sheep know the voice of their Shepherd. They know his voice of grace. They receive soul nourishment from his care. They experience eternal love and protection through his crucifixion and resurrection. They live within the safety and rest of his forgiveness and acceptance.[3] They know that their Shepherd-God, the sacrificial Lamb, laid down his life for the sheep and then took it up again to guide his sheep to his green pastures of grace, his living waters of mercy, in the land of his eternal rest.[4]

When you're lit up with love, you are inviting others to the green pastures and still waters of the Good Shepherd's love, protection, and nourishment. Every person is a precious sheep who has gone astray and is in desperate need of the Shepherd.[5] Our Shepherd Jesus loves his sheep with a loyal, forgiving, life-transforming, protective love. He refuses to abandon you, give up on you, or break his promises to you. Nothing can separate you from his loving grip of grace.[6]

The Good Shepherd loves his sheep and longs for us to know his heart. We know him, and he knows us. In the midst of the clamoring voices of the world, the cacophony of the wolves around us, we recognize his voice because we are his sheep. Our hearts are set to the beat of the rhythm of his grace.

Lost Sheep, Found Sheep

On the wall of my office is a picture of Jesus running after a lost lamb. The lamb is alone, covered in mud, terrified, and in danger. If only the lamb would turn around and see who is coming for her! Jesus leaves the ninety-nine sheep who are safe in the pen to chase down the one who is lost. He pursues us with grace, holding and securing us with his nail-pierced hands of mercy.[7] All of heaven is lit up with happiness when one sinner repents and turns to God's loving rest.[8] *When you're lit up with love, you help lost sheep turn around and see that the Good Shepherd is chasing them in his goodness and mercy.*

The more we know the Shepherd, the more we love and become like the One we know and love. And he is searching for his lost sheep. He loves to find them through you and me. We, the people of God, his church, the body of Christ, are on his search and rescue team.[9]

God's abundant life is available to whoever believes in King Jesus. Salvation means entering Jesus' Kingdom and abundant life, discovering that God's life has become our own.[10] As we participate in his life, we walk through doors the Holy Spirit opens to share the love and Good News about the Shepherd. *When you're lit up with love, you're not showing people a religion or an institution—you're excited to introduce them to Jesus, the risen Shepherd.*

We were created for a life of love, security, and nourishment in the Good Shepherd's care. Those of us who have entered the gate under the Shepherd's eternal supervision are now on mission,[11] searching for lost sheep in valleys and hills, bars and clubs, gyms and prisons, neighborhoods and schools and workplaces. Jesus runs after lost sheep through his found sheep. You and I get to invite precious, broken sheep into the Good Shepherd's green pastures and to quiet waters.

The world is full of lost sheep who are wandering in darkness, in danger, in exhaustion, in isolation. In Jesus, they can lay their heavy burdens down at the Cross. They can enter eternal rest.[12]

We share the gospel because we know the Shepherd's love. We've experienced his forgiveness and kindness—and we want others to know this Shepherd too. We proclaim to the lost sheep that our God has green pastures and quiet waters—come, be refreshed, be restored! The world's true Lord, the resurrected Messiah, the Good Shepherd, is inviting broken humanity to become whole in him, to come home and experience abundant life and rest in the Shepherd's Kingdom.[13]

This is the Good News our world is starving for.

Holy Habits

- *When you're lit up with love, you can introduce tired, lost sheep to the Good Shepherd, who can bring them to a place of refreshment and restoration.*

- *When you're lit up with love, you live in the confidence that Jesus, the Good Shepherd, is all that his sheep need.*

- *When you're lit up with love, you are inviting others to the green pastures and still waters of the Good Shepherd's love, protection, and nourishment.*

- *When you're lit up with love, you help lost sheep turn around and see that the Good Shepherd is chasing them in his goodness and mercy.*

- *When you're lit up with love, you're not showing people a religion or an institution—you're excited to introduce them to Jesus, the risen Shepherd.*

Reflection Questions

1. Is your soul fatigued? Why or why not? What seems to be making the people around you weary?

2. What do you think it means that Jesus is all that his sheep need? What are the implications for our everyday lives?

3. Jesus "refuses to abandon you, give up on you, or break his promises to you" (page 40). How does this truth make you feel?

4. What are some practical ways we can bring the love, comfort, and security of our Shepherd to lost sheep we encounter?

PRAYER

Jesus,

You are the Good Shepherd,

who lays his life down for his sheep.

Holy Spirit,

Empower me to join Jesus

on his mission of finding his lost sheep.

Father,

Fill me with eternal love.

May lost sheep hear and see your eternal love

in my life and my presentation of the gospel.

Amen.

CHAPTER 5

STARVED FOR HEALING

Meeting the God of Grace

Ann's parents divorced when she was five. That relational break created a wound in her that burrowed deep into her young soul, metastasizing over the years. Even though Ann would not have been able to verbalize her wound, her drive to be successful told the story of a girl who just wanted to be loved, valued, and seen.

Ann was the model of success—driven, ambitious, beautiful, and smart. She was an all-state athlete in high school and received athletic and academic scholarships to one of the top universities in America. She was a valedictorian in high school and at her university. In athletics, she ranked top twenty in the nation in her event. What no one knew was that Ann's drive for high achievement was a cry from her heart: *Don't leave me. I'm worth staying for.*

On the inside, intrusive thoughts told Ann that she was never good enough, pretty enough, skinny enough, or smart enough. Her obsession led to an eating disorder and poor decisions in relationships.

During her junior year in college, she met a guy. They became fast friends and fell in love. Shocking their parents, they got married in college. Ann and her husband, LaMont, were good friends, so their marriage was okay. He would say they were like close roommates who slept together and had things in common.

In those early years of marriage, Ann was slowly realizing that she could not *achieve* her way out of feeling inadequate and not worth staying for. She was also recognizing that guilt and shame were suffocating her soul.

At work, Ann met a woman named Karen and became intrigued by her faith. "Karen is a good Christian," she would tell LaMont. One day, Ann and Karen struck up a conversation while sipping coffee. Ann asked Karen, "Do you believe demons are real?"

Karen said, "Yes, I do." Then she asked Ann, "Are you a Christian?"

Ann responded, "Yeah, I believe in God."

Karen gently and clearly said, "Ann, being a Christian is more than believing in God. It means that you believe that Jesus died for your sins and rose from the dead. Have you placed your faith in Jesus doing this for you?" Karen continued sharing Jesus with Ann for months.

As a new parent, Ann thought that religion would be good for her baby daughter, so she decided to attend a church. She doesn't remember what the preacher preached on, but she does remember that at the end of the service, the choir sang and these words went straight to her heart: *Jesus died for me.* She started crying, grabbed her baby, and ran out of the church. As she drove home, a flood of tears streamed down her face. All she could think about was *Jesus died for me.*

Ann didn't know what had happened to her. But she knew that she was different.[1] She wanted her husband to experience the love and freedom from guilt and shame she was now experiencing. She wanted her husband to see life the way she was now seeing life. LaMont noticed an immediate change in Ann. And he liked it. Eventually, LaMont also met Jesus when a coworker clearly presented the gospel to him. And Jesus changed his life too.

Ann and LaMont left their successful corporate-America jobs and did the unimaginable: They started a church. People who knew Ann and LaMont from college could not believe these two irreligious, non-churchgoing people would become church planters! Ann and LaMont were so captivated by Jesus they wanted their family, their friends, and whomever else they met to know Jesus. This gospel passion led to them joining Jesus on his mission to reach lost people like them. They prayed that Jesus would use them to create a colorful church where people from different ethnic backgrounds would find community and unity in Jesus—a community where the brokenhearted, the forgotten, the left behind, the counted out, and the used and abused would experience the healing love of God in Christ.

The church that Vicki (Ann) Gray and Derwin (LaMont) Gray planted is called Transformation Church. As a result of two faithful believers sharing about Jesus in their workplace, Vicki and I came to Christ and planted a church that has seen thousands come to faith in Jesus.

Healing Grace

Our world is brutally competitive and relentlessly unforgiving. In a weary world, grace is an oasis in the desert.

Grace is not an abstract doctrine but a living, breathing person who lived a sinless life because we couldn't, who died the death we deserved on the cross, and who rose from the dead, ushering in a new creation.[2] Religion tells you what you must do to reach God; grace tells you what God has done to reach us.[3] Grace is Jesus doing what we could never do so we can become what we never imagined: participants in the very life of God.

We know something is not quite right with us. We crave something or someone to make the pain go away, to fill the void in our souls. That's why we work so hard to improve ourselves. Yet the harder we try, the more our flaws come into view. We don't know what we long for, but that longing is the loudest symptom of a life apart from God's extravagant love, his invitation to relationship.

Jesus is the one person who is honest about our broken condition: We are dead in sin, held captive by Satan, and sinners under judgment.[4] But Jesus doesn't leave us there. He sees us clearly and completely, and he meets us with grace. Jesus didn't tell us to heal our brokenness or clean ourselves up before he went to the cross! He went to the cross because we can't heal our brokenness or clean ourselves up.[5] The Cross of Christ carries our sins and heals our wounds.[6]

Grace is the unearned favor of God. Grace is the person of Jesus exchanging his life for yours. And because of grace, all that is true of Jesus is now true of you.[7] When God looks at you, he sees Jesus' sinless, God-glorifying life. Jesus' status before the Father is your status before the Father. The Father loves you as if you were his eternal Son because you are united with Jesus.[8] You now live because of his resounding victory over sin and death. The condemnation we rightly deserve has been condemned by Jesus. The death sentence we rightly deserve was served by Jesus. He died so we could be reborn in his resurrection life. Jesus is "grace upon grace."[9]

Because of God's grace, we experience *freedom* from sin and death, *friendship* with God, the *righteousness* of Christ, and the *sanctification* of growing in Christlikeness because we are in Christ.[10] People without Jesus need this kind of healing. And you have the medicine that makes sick souls whole.

Freedom (Redemption)

I love my children, and my deepest longing is that they would know Jesus and make him known. But my kids, like everyone else who has ever lived, were born with the Curse in their bones, the drive to try to live apart from God. As much as I love my children, nothing I do can ever free them from sin and death.

But I know who can free them: Jesus. Through Jesus' sacrifice and resurrection, he frees (redeems) all who give their life to him.[11]

One of the first echoes of Jesus' redemption for humanity is seen in the book of Exodus. God's chosen people, the nation of Israel, had spent four hundred years enslaved in Egypt, and God was set on their freedom. After Pharoah refused God's command multiple times,[12] God instructed the children of Israel to place the blood of an unblemished lamb (or goat) on the doorframes of their homes. As YHWH (God) brought judgment on Egypt, he would pass over the blood-marked homes.[13] Humbled and defeated, Pharaoh said to Moses, "Go, worship the LORD as you have requested."[14] The death of the lamb was the pathway to freedom.

In the same way, Jesus paid for our freedom with his life. He became the unblemished Lamb of God, who takes away the sins of the world. Grace costs us nothing, but it cost God everything.[15] That's how much he loves us.

Knowing Jesus is knowing freedom. As we become Christlike, or *holy*, through the Holy Spirit's power, we are freed from envy, pride, greed, and a whole host of other behaviors that strip humans of their genuine humanity. And through the unrelenting power of King Jesus, each of us can experience freedom from the fear of death.

Friendship (Reconciliation)

I had only been a follower of Jesus for a year when I met Gordon, who owned the barbershop where I'd get my hair cut. He was rough around the edges. Gordon was starving for the gospel even though he didn't know it. His words and actions were symptoms of a wounded soul. Spiritually, he had tried to heal himself—Gordon's faith was a combination of self-help guru and nation of Islam—but he didn't want anything to do with Jesus or Christianity (or as he called it, "the

White man's religion"). As I spent more time around Gordon, though, I knew Jesus wanted me to be good news to him.

Common ground is where the gospel can bear fruit, and golf was my common ground with Gordon. But playing golf with him was frustrating—Gordon was a cheating machine! Still, God made it clear to me: I was supposed to be present in Gordon's life, sow gospel seeds of grace, and just be prayerfully patient.

Over the years, the loud, angry man began to change. He was still loud, but grace defused his anger and bitterness. This once-hard man now cries at the mention of Jesus' name!

What happened? Gordon's self-made life crumbled. And Jesus met him in his pain. I didn't preach a gospel message to him—the Good News just infused our everyday conversations about life, business, marriage, and race. And Gordon discovered the gift of reconciliation to God. God became his friend. Gordon became God's friend.

Reconciliation means that the hostility between God and man has ended, the great divide that separated God and man has been closed by the blood of Jesus. The God of grace is relentless in his pursuit of his image bearers; he longs to make us his eternal friends.[16] God's motivation for reconciliation is always love, and he delights in making our relationship with him whole again.[17] In reconciliation, God is not trying to reform people with bad behavior or to clean us up enough so we can be around him. No—his grace transforms us into a brand-new creation. Every saint has a past, and every sinner can have a beautiful future in the reconciling arms of God.[18] *When you're lit up with love, you invite enemies to become friends of God.*[19]

As Jesus' friends,[20] as we follow him in faith, we begin to look more and more like him:

- Bitterness turns into forgiveness.
- Hate is replaced with love.

- Apathy is replaced with compassion.
- Death dies, and we become more alive than we ever knew possible.

Reconciliation is Jesus' hope for humanity.[21] Our hearts are not designed to carry bitterness and unforgiveness. Reconciliation purges our souls, removing the toxicity that destroys us and replacing it with a love that overflows out of our relationship with God and into the rest of our lives. That's what happened with me and Gordon. A once-difficult relationship has blossomed into a life-giving friendship. We both were reconciled to God in Christ, and we were reconciled to each other.

Broken and weary people need to know of this God who invites them into reconciled, whole relationship. *When you're lit up with love, you know you have been reconciled to God by Christ and now have the sacred responsibility to invite others to be reconciled to the God who hungers to forgive sins and be in relationship with his people.*

God and God alone has closed the divide that separates us from him.

God and God alone has reset the fracture that broke our relationship with him.

God and God alone can give you the power to be a reconciler.

Righteousness (Justification)

Imagine that you are sitting in a chair in front of God the Father, all his glory is blazing in unapproachable light, and Jesus, in his blood-soaked robe, is sitting in a chair next to you. An angel asks God the Father, "Who is more righteous, Jesus or this image bearer?"

How do you think God the Father would answer?

Because of the life, death, and resurrection of Jesus Christ, and because you have placed your faith in him, God the Father would say,

"They are equally righteous because _____ [*your name*] is 'in' my Son. I see all those who are in my beloved Son the same way I see him: as perfectly righteous." In Christ, you are holy and are without fault in God's eyes. Not only is your sin removed, but God has also given you his own righteousness.[22] The sinless life Jesus lived, which fulfilled the law, is now applied to you.

What changes when you see yourself through the righteousness of Christ, holy and faultless in the eyes of God? Guilt and shame are powerless. Your salvation and your eternal destiny in the new heaven and new earth is secure. No mistake or failure can change who God has declared you to be. You are free from condemnation![23]

Embracing God's righteousness in Christ as my own righteousness transformed my life. Before I understood the righteousness of God, I was a compulsive stutterer afraid of public speaking. I believe my stuttering was a trauma response. But now I am a pastor. What happened? My security in God's love became unshakable. Nothing, not even the trauma I had experienced, could overcome my new identity. I gained a new confidence, a new power, a new mind, and a new way to relate to the world. When I began to see myself as God sees me in Christ,[24] by faith, in the Spirit's power, I no longer allowed my past pain and trauma to define me. Jesus alone defines me!

The same Jesus who declares me righteousness can declared you righteous too. If Jesus could transform me, he could do it for anyone! *When you're lit up with love, you become a recipient of God's righteousness and invite others to share in the righteousness of Jesus.*

As you share Christ with the people you meet, people who are weary and burdened from trying to heal their own wounds, let them know about the righteous-making power in the blood of Jesus.[25] Jesus is not looking for people who are weary from trying to make themselves acceptable to God. He's looking for weary people who know they can't.

Sanctification (Growing in Christlikeness)

The God of immeasurable grace who declares his people righteous also enables his Holy Spirit–inhabited people to *live righteously* as we obey Jesus' loving initiatives in our lives.[26] This life of holiness is called *progressive sanctification*. As the Holy Spirit forms us to become more and more like Jesus, we shed selfishness for selflessness, pride for humility, dishonesty for honesty, and impatience for patience. Sanctification is the lifelong process of being formed into the image of Jesus and being restored to our original, God-exalting glory.[27] When we fail to allow the Holy Spirit to do this work, we are robbing ourselves, our family, the world, and the Kingdom of God of what Jesus wants to do in us.

Sanctification is the beautiful struggle to become in *practice* what God declares us to be by our *position* in Christ. The new life in Christ we have received and are pointing others to is so much more than a Get out of Jail Free card. As we are sanctified, God the Father graciously reparents us through the broken places and promises and the other hurts we've accumulated in life. Jesus leads us with his love, guides us with his wisdom, and sustains us with his strength as we daily surrender to the Spirit's loving presence.

Grace Formed

The blood of Jesus is powerful enough to free us from slavery to sin; to forgive our past, present, and future sins; to heal the wounds we have inflicted and the wounds we carry. Grace forms us into new people who live in new ways. I know because the grace of Jesus changed my life.

My father was nineteen when I was born. I suspect he suffered from mental-health issues and substance abuse. But I didn't know that until I was much older. I have more empathy for him now. As a teenager, I didn't. His absence in my life hurt.

At thirteen, I decided I didn't need him. I was going to be successful without him. My anger toward him was like burning coal fueling an engine.

But when anger is your fuel, your success pollutes your soul and those around you. Toxic is toxic, even if it looks good externally.

Around 2001, a few years after I had become a follower of Jesus, I was writing letters to family and friends about how forgiving and loving Jesus is and how he could transform their lives. As I wrote, I heard a voice say, "Go find your father."

I don't know for sure if it was God's voice, but the next thing I knew, I was on my office floor in a puddle of tears, cussing and shouting, "My father doesn't *deserve* me finding him. Where was he when I was sexually molested? Where was he when I needed to learn how to treat women? Where was he when I needed him? He doesn't deserve me finding him!"

The Healer gave me time to be honest about my pain. Then it was almost like he picked me up, put me on his lap, and said, "Son, I feel all your pain. On the cross my Son took it all upon himself. I hurt with you. And I can heal you. Derwin, it's true—your father does not deserve you finding and forgiving him. But never forget: You didn't deserve my Son, Jesus, finding and forgiving you."

In that moment, even though I didn't want to, I knew I needed to find my father and forgive him.

After I discovered he was in prison, I wrote him a short letter: "Dad, I want you to know that I forgive you and I love you. I want you to be part of my life. You have two wonderful grandchildren you need to know."

One afternoon when I checked the mail, his response had arrived. I ran into the house and sprinted up to my office. Trying to read the letter through tears was difficult. But he wrote something I had never heard him say: "Son, thank you for forgiving me. I want to know my grandchildren. And I love you."

I just wept. The redeeming blood of Jesus *freed* me from being held hostage in the prison of unforgiveness, haunted by intrusive thoughts of revenge. Because God's grace was forming me into the image of Jesus, the Holy Spirit empowered me to offer that grace to my father. Forgiving someone who hurt you doesn't mean that you continue to let them hurt you. Forgiveness means that the person who hurt you no longer lives in your emotions and reactions, no longer reinjures you because you're no longer reliving the pain. Remember, grace is freedom.

God graciously gives wounded people a new, grace-formed identity that secures them in the grips of his kindness, empowering them to live and share in his abundant life:

- **Grace-formed people have the eyes to see broken, hurting, lost people** who need Jesus' grace as much as we do. When Jesus rescued me from my mess, I immediately wanted other messy people to meet Jesus too. I felt their pain, I lived their confusion, and I knew their regret. I knew if they could just see Jesus—not religion or a bad church experience—they, too, would fall in love with him. That's what grace does. It wins your heart and moves your hands to reach others! *When you're lit up with love, you make the grace of God a priority when talking to people who don't know him.* Everyone needs grace. No sin is too strong for God's powerful arms of love.

- **Grace-formed people exhibit the kindness of grace.** God's kindness is what leads people to repentance.[28] We get to bring that kindness to the people we meet because through the gospel of grace, we are "in Christ": our life and his are eternally interwoven in an unbreakable bond of love. *When you're lit up with love, you are inviting people into Christ himself.* Everything that is true of Jesus becomes true of those who follow him. We approach wounded people with Jesus' kindness, letting them know they can come to Jesus as they are—and he will re-create them into a masterpiece![29]

- **Grace-formed people live differently.** We're not caught up in the dysfunctions of our emotionally unwell, weary culture. *When you're lit up with love, you live at the pace of grace.* Good-News people refuse to live under the tyranny of the urgent. In response to God's invitation of life, we intentionally cultivate healthy rhythms of grace like a day of delight and rest (Sabbath), Scripture reading, prayer, community, silence, service, and confession. How we live becomes an act of resistance against consumerism and hustle culture. We offer a nonanxious, peaceful presence that soothes the exhausted souls of those around us.[30] A life of peace and emotional health amid chaos bears witness to the resurrection life of Christ. A healthy life lived at the pace of grace is an evangelistic strategy.

I suspect many in modern society are not rejecting the Jesus of Scripture but a poor representation of him. Friend, the God who heals us with grace is beautiful and life-giving. Jesus wants us to share and live in his God-glorifying life.[31] *When you're lit up with love, you are inviting people into a Jesus-saturated, Jesus-immersed, Jesus-reliant life.*

Holy Habits

- *When you're lit up with love, you invite enemies to become friends of God.*

- *When you're lit up with love, you know you have been reconciled to God by Christ and now have the sacred responsibility to invite others to be reconciled to the God who hungers to forgive sins and be in relationship with his people.*

- *When you're lit up with love, you become a recipient of God's righteousness and invite others to share in the righteousness of Jesus.*

- *When you're lit up with love, you make the grace of God a priority when talking to people who don't know him.*

- *When you're lit up with love, you are inviting people into Christ himself.*

- *When you're lit up with love, you live at the pace of grace.*

- *When you're lit up with love, you are inviting people into a Jesus-saturated, Jesus-immersed, Jesus-reliant life.*

Reflection Questions

1. How have you experienced God's grace in your life?

2. What are some ways you've seen sin imprison people? How would you express the freedom from sin that God has given you?

3. Have you encountered someone who seems hostile toward God? What wounds or brokenness do you sense they may be living with? What are some ways you can be a friend to them to demonstrate the friendship of God?

4. Do you see yourself as righteous? If not, how might truly believing that you have been given Christ's own righteousness change your thinking, confidence, and way of relating to the world?

5. What have you noticed about your journey of sanctification so far? What do you sense God wanting to shape in you right now?

6. Consider the postures, motives, and actions of grace-formed people. Which do you want to grow in?

PRAYER

Holy Spirit,

Moment by moment, day by day,

remind me of who I am and whose I am.

In Christ, I am a new creation,

eternally loved, alive with the resurrection life of King Jesus.

I am redeemed.

I am forgiven.

I am righteous.

I am God's friend.

King Jesus,

You have given us the ministry of reconciliation.

You laid down your life and took it back up

so the unrighteous can be made righteous,

so enemies can become friends,

so the dead can live,

so the unforgiven can be forgiven.

Father,

Send me on mission

and give me success in reaching people with your grace.

Amen.

CHAPTER 6

STARVED FOR NEW LIFE

Getting in the Transformation Game

In 1988, my high school defensive back coach changed the trajectory of my life. During my senior football season at Judson High School in Converse, Texas, my playing was good but not great. Somehow I started to inhale the toxin called entitlement, which poisoned my heart and clouded my mind until one day I decided to skip practice.

If you missed practice at my school, you had better be sick or have been abducted by a UFO. (I was neither.) When I showed up at practice the next day, I found out that I had been demoted from the starting defensive unit. In Friday's game I didn't play, and we won 45–0. The following Monday, my coach asked me to stay after practice so he could talk to me.

"Dewey," he said, "you can be great. But you are not giving me your all. I'm not going to let you play unless you give me your all." Tears were tumbling down his face.

I joined him in crying, and he continued, "You can play football in college and make something of yourself. I have your future in my hands. It's up to you to decide if you want to be great."

Coach cared enough to call out what was beneath my missing practice: my own selfishness. He didn't allow me to have a pity party—he challenged me to become responsible and selfless. He didn't allow me to give up—he called me to live up to my talent.

The rest of the week I practiced harder than I had ever practiced.

Come game time on Friday, when the starting defensive unit went out on the field, I was on the sideline. At this point, I figured I had blown my chances to play college football.

But on the second play of the game, my coach yelled, "Dewey, get in the game!" I sprinted on the field like a bolt of lightning. I played that game and the rest of my senior season with an unrelenting passion to be great for my team. At the end of the season, we were state champs, I was voted a first-team all-state player, and I received a football scholarship to Brigham Young University.

Coach Mike Sullivan changed my life. He loved me enough to challenge me, bringing out greatness that I didn't even know was in me. Because of that love, I matured as a student, a leader, and a young man getting ready to leave home for college. And I'm forever grateful.

Ten years went by. Coach called me to talk about football and my NFL career with the Carolina Panthers, but I told him, "Coach, something has happened to me. I must tell you about my new relationship with Jesus." For the next several minutes he listened. Then he said, "Dewey, I need you to come to Texas as soon as you can." Vicki, our baby girl, and I boarded a plane and flew to Texas.

I met him at the new school where he was employed. We sat down in his office just like we did in 1988, but now the roles were reversed. With tears tumbling down his face once more, he said, "Son, I lost my marriage. I've made a lot of mistakes. I need forgiveness. I want what you have. Will you coach me in the spiritual life the way I coached you in football?"

I shared the gospel with him. I told him he could be forgiven and that he could experience God's love. And that in Christ, God's will gives him the righteousness of Christ. No more guilt, no more shame. He could have a new life.

We held hands and prayed Romans 10:9-10: "If you confess with your mouth, 'Jesus is Lord,' and believe in your heart that God raised him from the dead, you will be saved. One believes with the heart, resulting in righteousness, and one confesses with the mouth, resulting in salvation" (csb). Coach has followed Jesus ever since.

The only thing greater than receiving new life from Jesus is helping someone else discover the transformed life Jesus offers.

Brought to Life . . .

It'd be futile to walk through a cemetery and shout over the headstones, "You are forgiven!" A dead body in a coffin can't hear! That's what it would be like if Jesus only gave people forgiveness without also giving them new life. When we come to Jesus by grace through faith, Jesus doesn't just make our lives a little better or help us be a bit more moral: He resurrects our sin-dead selves into a completely new, transformed life that increasingly reflects who he is.[1]

What is this transformed life? At the moment when we believe the gospel, we experience regeneration, or new birth in Christ. By an act of unimaginable grace, we become participants in the resurrection life of Jesus.[2] We are eternally united to the One who walked out of the tomb, leaving it empty, so our empty life could be filled with his.[3]

> You also were included in Christ when you heard the
> message of truth, the gospel of your salvation. When you
> believed, you were marked in him with a seal, the promised
> Holy Spirit, who is a deposit guaranteeing our inheritance
> until the redemption of those who are God's possession—
> to the praise of his glory.
> EPHESIANS 1:13-14, NIV

In Christ, we are transferred from spiritual death to spiritual life. We are no longer dead in Adam; we are alive in Christ.[4] Because the

Messiah's life becomes our life, he awakens new dreams, new abilities, and a new moral character in us.

- My new life in Christ changed my dreams from working at an investment firm to planting Transformation Church.

- My new life in Christ turned a kid who only scored a 16 on his ACT into a New Testament scholar.

- My new life in Christ has transformed my character. I am not who I used to be, and I am not who I am going to be. Thank God Jesus is still working on me.

When I played for the Indianapolis Colts, I befriended a local sports reporter. He considered himself a good person who had just a few things he needed to work on—he and God were "good," he figured. After years of conversation, I shared with my friend that Jesus was not interested in making him better—Jesus wanted to make him alive.

"What do you mean?" he asked. I read Ephesians 2:1-4 and John 3:5 with him, showing him that our problem is that we are spiritually dead, estranged from God, and under judgment because we all fall short of the glory of God.[5] He started crying. He said, "What can I do?"

I told him, "You can't do anything but give your life to Jesus so he can give you his life. Do you want his life? Do you want his forgiveness?"

He said yes. Twenty-seven years later, he is still walking with Jesus—and so is his family. *When you're lit up with love, you want to see everyone around you brought to life with Jesus' life.*

Why did Jesus sacrifice himself to raise us from the pit of spiritual death and give us spiritual life? What does it look like to live by faith in Christ so he can live through us? We are brought to life to be storytellers, glory reflectors, and world changers.

. . . to Be Storytellers

Being brought back to life is a pretty good story, isn't it? And people are hardwired for story. Sharing the story of how Jesus brought you from death to life will always be a powerful way to plant gospel seeds in a person's soul.

Part of my story is that I used to be afraid of death. When I went to my grandfather's funeral as a little boy, everyone was crying and screaming. From then on, death scared me. There was no hope. There was no Good News.

But then I learned that Jesus freed me from the fear of death—I learned that in him, through his death-defeating death and resurrection, death was no longer my destiny. Jesus now has the last word, not death. This belief is not a matter of willpower; the Spirit assures us that it's true.[6] I'm no longer afraid.

Jesus also freed me and *is freeing me* from toxic and unhealthy habits, death to my soul and spirit. I tried to change myself and couldn't. But when I embraced Jesus, he took all my death and gave me his life, complete with a new heart and new power. I'm not perfect (nor will I ever be), but daily his grace is making me more like him. With the life of Christ in you, you have a story to tell: *his-story* of rescuing you. It doesn't have to be complicated. In fact, the most powerful stories are simple, personal, clear, scriptural, and invitational. *When you're lit up with love, you live out of new life you have been given—and are eager to share that life with those who don't know Jesus.*

. . . to Be Glory Reflectors

God's rescue plan through the Messiah is so much more than for us to escape hell or even go to heaven when we die. It is indeed good news that Jesus saves us from an eternity separated from God. And yes, those of us in Christ will spend eternity with him in the new heaven and new earth with glorified, resurrected bodies. But just as Jesus saves us *from* wrath, death, and judgment, he also saves us *for* something. Being "in Christ" means we have been transformed, brought out of death and into life. Because we have seen our lives change, we know how much God longs to do that for others.

When you're lit up with love, you are convinced that the gospel has the power to transform the lives of people who have yet to encounter the saving love of God in Christ because the gospel has transformed your life. We are offering people what they were created for: the glory of God. We glorify God when Jesus is our supreme delight, when his character begins to become our character. Humanity was created to embody the glory of God.[7] *When you're lit up with love, you know that salvation is the restoration of God's intended purpose for humans: to be glory reflectors.*[8]

People in Christ, in response to him "[giving] himself for us to redeem us from all wickednesss and to purify for himself a people that are his very own,"[9] become energized to glorify our Father in heaven by doing good on earth. And the ultimate good is introducing people to the God of goodness.[10]

As we behold Jesus, he takes hold of us. And day by day, in the rocky terrain of life—in the dark valleys, on the sunny mountaintops—we begin to reflect him. God desires for our lives to become a living portrait of heaven on earth.[11] And that portrait of grace looks like a life of "love, joy, peace, patience, kindness, goodness, faithfulness, gentleness, and self-control."[12] A genuine human life was meant to exhibit these Spirit-enabled virtues. Jesus wants to restore our genuine humanity, so much so that he takes up residence in us to accomplish it.[13]

God's Good News is that dead people can be made alive, transformed into light bringers and glory reflectors in a dark world. As Good-News people, we get to invite people to become who they were meant to be—and to experience the abundant life they were created for.

... to Be World Changers

Men and women made alive by Jesus can change the world. Seriously. Our new birth unleashes a new power in us: God chooses to inhabit his people, lighting them up with his love and glory. We see this throughout the history of our faith. Take eighteenth-century cleric John Wesley, for example. John embodied external religion for much of his early life—until May 24, 1738, when he experienced new birth in the power of God. Here's how he describes meeting Jesus:

> I went very unwillingly to a society in Aldersgate Street, where one was reading Luther's preface to the Epistle to the Romans. About a quarter before nine, while the leader was describing the change which God works in the heart through faith in Christ, I felt my heart strangely warmed. I felt I did trust in Christ alone for salvation; and an assurance was given me that He had taken away my sins, even mine, and saved me from the law of sin and death.[14]

From that moment on, John Wesley was lit up with love, and King Jesus used his life to start a revival that reached across the Atlantic! John preached salvation by grace through faith, new birth, justification, and holiness, and those truths moved people from death-dealing superficial religion to alive-in-Jesus transformation. In a time when many White people professed to follow Christ while enslaving Black people, John Wesley saw clearly that slavery was evil and anti-gospel. Wesley scholar Fred Sanders writes, "Wesley condemned slavery repeatedly from the pulpit and used his personal influence against it wherever he could."[15]

When Jesus makes you alive, you don't just think differently; you also spend the rest of your life ministering to see God's Good News change the broken places and systems of our world. John Wesley lived out his gospel convictions until the end of his days. Shortly before his death, he wrote this to British politician William Wilberforce:

> Unless God has raised you up for this very thing [opposing slavery], you will be worn out by the opposition of men and devils. But if God be for you, who can be against you? Are all of them together stronger than God? O be not weary of well doing! Go on, in the name of God and in the power of his might, till even American slavery (the vilest that ever saw the sun) shall vanish away before it.[16]

The gospel not only breaks spiritual chains—it dismantles physical ones too. The work of Christians like John Wesley and William Wilberforce led to the dismantling of slavery in England and eventually in America! John Wesley became a world changer because Jesus gave him a new heart, a new mind, and new eyes to see God's longings for his people.

We are people who have been brought out of death and into life, out of darkness and into the marvelous light. Our whole selves have been radically transformed. That means we live and move through the world with the Kingdom of God as our compass. We can't stop talking about what God has done. We can't help but reflect his glory to the people around us. And in small and big ways, we become people who can't be held back from trying to change the world in ways that reflect the heart of God.

Holy Habits

- *When you're lit up with love, you want to see everyone around you brought to life with Jesus' life.*

- *When you're lit up with love, you live out of new life you have been given—and are eager to share that life with those who don't know Jesus.*

- *When you're lit up with love, you are convinced that the gospel has the power to transform the lives of people who have yet to encounter the saving love of God in Christ because the gospel has transformed your life.*

- *When you're lit up with love, you know that salvation is the restoration of God's intended purpose for humans: to be glory reflectors.*

Reflection Questions

1. What are some aspects of your old self that have died?

2. What are some specific new dreams, abilities, and aspects of moral character Jesus has awakened in you?

3. Write out your death-to-life story, including of Jesus' ongoing transforming work in you. What do you notice? How might your story invite someone else into new life with God?

4. How might the people you see on a regular basis need to experience God's glory? What would it look like for you to reflect that glory through your words, actions, motives, and thoughts?

5. Consider some of the broken realities of our world that you care deeply about. How could you be a world changer as you carry the light of God's Good News?

PRAYER

Father,

You are life. I was dead.

Thank you for bringing me to life in the life of Christ.

King Jesus,

May I delight in and adore you so much

that you are my supreme passion.

Holy Spirit,

Give me power to be a great gospel storyteller,

glory reflector, and world changer.

In Jesus' name,

amen.

PART THREE

LIT UP WITH LOVE

CHAPTER 7

EVERYDAY MISSIONARIES

Stepping into Your Calling

The year was 1993. I'd been drafted by the Indianapolis Colts and had just started living out my NFL dreams when I observed something strange after practice one day. After getting out of the shower, one of my teammates wrapped a towel around his waist, grabbed a Bible, and began to ask people in the locker room, "Do you know Jesus?"

My first thought was, *Bro, do you know you are half naked?* Out of curiosity, I asked a veteran on the team, "What's up with the dude asking people if they know Jesus?"

My teammate said, "Don't pay attention to him. That's the Naked Preacher!" And that was my first introduction to Steve Grant.

Steve was a tenth-round draft pick by the Indianapolis Colts in 1992. He played college ball at West Virginia University. He started going to a Bible study on campus because he heard the head coach would be there. Steve wasn't into Jesus, but he wanted to impress his coach.

On week three of the Bible study, something changed. As Steve listened to the gospel being proclaimed, Jesus claimed his heart. His life was never the same.

As Steve spent more time being discipled by other Christians, he started to see himself as a missionary. Before the 1992 NFL Draft, he had only one request of God: *I do not want to play for the Green Bay Packers or the Indianapolis Colts.* After the Colts drafted him, Steve knew God was sending him to the Colts not only to be a great football player but also to be a missionary. He said, "I vow to reach as many of my teammates and coaches as possible with the gospel."

One day, as I was sitting at my locker, I saw the Naked Preacher walking toward me. *Oh no, here comes that religious guy,* I thought.

That's when he asked me a question that forever transformed my life: "Rookie D. Gray, do you know Jesus?"

For the next five years, Steve helped me discover who Jesus is and what he'd done for me. On August 2, 1997, while the Colts were in training camp at Anderson University in Anderson, Indiana, I found myself walking alone to my dorm room with an overwhelming sense of God's presence. Suddenly, I knew I needed forgiveness. I knew I needed love that was unconditional, not based on how good or bad I was. I knew football was not big enough to heal my hurts, cover my shame, or silence the voice of blame—I needed a divine purpose to fill the empty space in my soul.

The light switch had been turned on. I believed in Jesus. I was born again. God's love lit me up from the inside out.

When I got to my dorm room, I called my wife and told her, "I want to be more committed to you, and I want to be committed to Jesus." After our conversation, I just wept. How could Jesus love and forgive someone like me? In an instant, I was a new man, in a new family, and in a new Kingdom, with a new power and purpose. Surrounded by the teammates I used to mock for their faith in Christ, I was baptized by Steve in a hotel swimming pool the night before a game.

All this happened because the Naked Preacher took Jesus' words to go make disciples seriously.[1]

You Are an Everyday Missionary

Steve saw himself as an everyday missionary right where he was. He wasn't just a Christian who happened to be in that locker room; he saw that locker room as his mission field. Reaching his lost teammates was his priority.

Did you know that God has sent you to your school, gym, neighborhood, or job so you can be a missionary? The moment you said yes to Jesus as your Savior, your sins were forgiven, you received new life, and Jesus gave you the ministry and mission of reconciliation.

When you're lit up with love, you know your career is a conduit of your calling: missionary. As you delight in the wondrous grace of King Jesus, a holy awareness of his presence and his heart to reach lost people shape you to have a heart like his.[2]

Jesus was lit up with love on earth because *he is love*. He left the splendors of eternity and entered time and space to seek and save the lost.[3] Now that he has ascended back to the right hand of the Father and reigns on his throne, he lights you up with love so you can leverage your time, talents, and treasures as you live on mission with him.

Terry, an original member of Transformation Church, personifies being an everyday missionary. He works in IT and sees his job as a means of being the presence of Christ in the workplace. Because of his faith, he works with excellence and conducts himself with integrity, and people feel safe to confide in him. Bringing the presence of Christ to his work has allowed Terry to sow gospel seeds into his coworkers' lives for years.

You can do the same. Approach every day, wherever you are—in your workplace, your kids' schools, your gym—in the power and presence of Christ, and he will light you up with love.

When you're lit up with love, you are compelled by the love of Christ to leverage your life as an everyday missionary.[4] Because you know the hope, comfort, healing, and transformation of Jesus in your own life, you want everyone else to know it too. You can't help but join Jesus on his mission to rescue the lost.

If you are anything like me, you might feel intimidated about sharing your faith. That's natural—even if we are rooted in the love of God, even if we understand people's deep need to experience reconciliation. I experience the fear of rejection often when I'm telling someone about Jesus. I think, *What if they hate me? What if they think I'm weird?* During those times, I have to preach to myself, *Derwin, love people as best you can. And remember, if someone rejects the message, they are not rejecting you.* We share Jesus with people to sow gospel seeds, not to get results. God handles the results.

When you're lit up with love, you don't feel the weight of results because you know you are proclaiming Jesus as King and Savior of humanity—and it's not your message but his.[5] When you know it's Jesus' message and not yours, fear fades. The beauty, hope, and urgency of the gospel message overcome.

It may take years for people to come to faith in Christ. It took me five! But consider what happens when we walk by faith and choose to lay aside our fears and introduce people around us to Jesus. When the gospel takes root, marriages are healed, people on the verge of suicide live, relationships are restored, and new ministries start. The gospel creates endless possibilities of love.

The Naked Preacher was not ashamed of the gospel, nor did he allow fear of being made fun of silence him. My life is a testament to God's work and Steve's choice to be an everyday missionary. Transformation Church has become a beautiful multiethnic, Jesus-focused community of thirteen thousand people. We have seen nearly nine thousand people come to faith in Christ; we started a free grocery market and have provided over a million meals for people in need;

we've canceled over sixteen million dollars in medical debt for people in the Carolinas; we've trained over six hundred pastors; and we've planted a church in Madrid, Spain, and helped plant many more.

How does this kind of exponential overflow of God's love happen? Through the Good News of Jesus and through the people Jesus uses to spread that Good News. Only in eternity will I know the full effect of Steve gospelizing me: the ripple effect of lives changed because one man chose to persist in sharing Jesus with those around him.

Steve loves Jesus. And his love for Jesus changed my life—eternally. So many other lives have also been changed as a result of his obedience to join Jesus on mission. What could happen if you let God minister through you as an instrument of grace? What lives might change if you decided to become an everyday missionary, sharing the story of what God has done for you, right where you are? Can you imagine the difference the people you share Christ with will make as a result of you sowing gospel seeds in their lives? That excites me. Does it excite you?

When you're lit up with love, you know that Jesus changes lives through people whose lives have been changed by him—and you're ready to join him in that mission.

Five Ways of Being an Everyday Missionary

I had finally found my wife a good used SUV online, about forty-five minutes from where we lived. After a test drive and a little negotiation, we were ready to sign the paperwork. That's when one of the employees asked, "What do you do?"

"My wife and I started a church called Transformation Church in 2010," I said.

Then he said, "My wife and I have been talking about going to church. Why did you start one?"

I told him, "We grew up not attending church or knowing

anything about Jesus. My entire life was based on how good I was at football. But even when I made it to the NFL, the fulfillment I thought I would have never arrived. I also knew I needed forgiveness for things I had done. And I struggled as a husband. Because I was afraid of being hurt, I couldn't fully love my wife, which left her feeling neglected. And I knew one day my professional football career would end—then who would I be? That scared me. But a teammate told me the greatest news I had ever heard: that the unconditional love, forgiveness, and fulfillment I was looking for was found in Jesus. Eventually he led me to faith in Christ. And my life has never been the same."

He said, "What's the name of your church again? My wife and I are coming."

Jesus sends us on mission in the everydayness of life. Gospel opportunities abound; we only need to attune our hearts to the Holy Spirit's promptings to see them. *When you're lit up with love, you are prayed up and prepared to share the gospel with clarity, in a way that meets people where they are.* Being an everyday missionary—like the Naked Preacher—doesn't require a theology degree or a certain kind of personality. It simply requires us to show up in our contexts in five ordinary ways:

1. **Be Christ Centered**: The Naked Preacher was captivated by Jesus and his gospel. With every fiber of his being, he wanted others to know and love Jesus. This type of passion only comes from being with Jesus, marinating in his grace, soaking in his loving-kindness, relying on the Holy Spirit's power.

    Everyday missionaries are Christ centered. Their message is "to know nothing among you except Jesus Christ and him crucified."[6] A Christ-centered, everyday missionary begins the day praying to Jesus, thinking of Jesus, following Jesus, and listening for the Holy Spirit's leading in the interactions that occur throughout the day. Everyday missionaries stay in step with God, preparing for future gospel conversations so when the time is right, they are ready.

2. **Be Consistent:** The Naked Preacher showed up every day as the same person. He was not an emotional roller coaster. One time a teammate threw a wad of tape aimed at another player, but it hit the Naked Preacher in the eye. He looked at the player and said, "If I didn't love Jesus, I would hurt you." He was walking in the Holy Spirit's power, displaying self-control and peace.[7] Steve was able to respond consistently from a gospel-soaked stance.

   Everyday missionaries are consistent. Their lives progressively mirror Jesus, regardless of who they're talking to or what's happening. They are consistent because they are spiritually and emotionally healthy. They know their lives may be the only Bible that someone reads, so they take their own discipleship seriously. A consistent public life is the fruit of a consistent private life of prayer, Scripture reading, and meditation on their identity in Christ.

3. **Be Clear:** The Naked Preacher was clear, patient, and straightforward in his gospel presentation. He shared how Jesus forgave, restored, and reconciled us to God and each other through his life, death, and resurrection.

   Everyday missionaries are clear. In a world with so much noise and so many distractions, a clear, focused presentation of Jesus goes a long way in reaching people with the gospel. Being crystal clear means that you share *who Jesus is* (the sinless Son of God and true Lord of the universe), *what he came to do* (die for the sins of the world and be raised from the dead), and *how people can give their lives to him by faith* (by believing that Jesus died for their sins and was resurrected from the dead, defeating sin and death).

4. **Be Cross-Cultural:** The Naked Preacher is Black, and he was committed to the multiethnic, multigenerational power of the gospel. He shared the gospel with everyone on the team: White, Black, Latino, Asian—it didn't matter! He reminds me of the Jewish "men from Cyprus and Cyrene, who came to Antioch and began speaking to the Greeks also, proclaiming the good news about the Lord Jesus."[8]

    Everyday missionaries are cross-cultural. When you're lit up with love, you cross ethnic and class boundaries to proclaim the reconciling love of King Jesus. Because the Good News is for all people, it is critical that we learn how to be curious and intentional when connecting with people from diverse backgrounds. For example, the apostle Paul used different approaches to sharing the gospel depending on who he was speaking with. With his Jewish kinsmen, he started with the Old Testament and how Jesus is the fulfillment of the law, the promised Messiah.[9] When sharing the gospel with Gentiles, Paul started with Creation and moved to God's self-revelation of Jesus as the world's true Lord and Savior.[10]

5. **Be Compassionate:** Whenever one of my teammates had a problem, they were at the Naked Preacher's locker, receiving counsel. He was compassionate and patient, no matter what someone's life and choices looked like. How do I know? Because he was compassionate and patient with me.

    Everyday missionaries are compassionate. Everyone around us is hurting, but most people are too busy to notice. Everyday missionaries, though, are on high alert for the needs of other human beings. They are praying and prepared to notice people in pain. Just slow down and ask God to give you eyes to see: The Holy Spirit will give you the ability to hear and sense people in need.

When you have inhaled God's grace, sharing your faith becomes a spiritual exhale. You've experienced the goodness of being with Jesus, and you want others to be with him too. *When you're lit up with love, you become the gospel wherever you are, living a life of love, humility, forgiveness, grace, and holiness.* May you be lit up with love so others can receive the light and be rescued from the darkness.

Holy Habits

- *When you're lit up with love, you know your career is a conduit of your calling: missionary.*

- *When you're lit up with love, you are compelled by the love of Christ to leverage your life as an everyday missionary.*

- *When you're lit up with love, you don't feel the weight of results because you know you are proclaiming Jesus as King and Savior of humanity—and it's not your message but his.*

- *When you're lit up with love, you know that Jesus changes lives through people whose lives have been changed by him—and you're ready to join him in that mission.*

- *When you're lit up with love, you are prayed up and prepared to share the gospel with clarity, in a way that meets people where they are.*

- *When you're lit up with love, you cross ethnic and class boundaries to proclaim the reconciling love of King Jesus.*

- *When you're lit up with love, you become the gospel wherever you are, living a life of love, humility, forgiveness, grace, and holiness.*

Reflection Questions

1. Where in your life do you regularly interact with lost people? If you can't think of a place, what are some activities or contexts where you can intentionally choose to be present and get to know people who don't know Jesus?

2. What lives might change if you decide to become an everyday missionary, sharing the story of what God has done for you, right where you are?

3. Which of the five ways of being an everyday missionary comes most naturally to you? Which one intimidates you? How might rooting yourself more in God's love or reflecting more on the needs of those around you address that intimidation?

4. How are you tempted to perform when it comes to sharing the gospel—either in how you share it or in how you don't? How does remembering that the gospel is about Jesus, not you, encourage you to see and do things differently?

PRAYER

Father,

Light me up with your love.

King Jesus,

You are the Light of the World.

May your grace burn brightly in me

so the world can see your face in mine.

Holy Spirit,

You have given me the message of reconciliation.

Send me on mission to reach the lost.

Give me favor!

Amen.

CHAPTER 8

EVERYTHING THAT HINDERS

Overcoming Our Barriers to Sharing Good News

The moment had arrived. My wife and I had built a relationship with our neighbor and her son for years. Our neighbor had let us know early in our relationship that she was from the Northeast and "people in the Northeast don't talk about religion." All sorts of barriers were staring me in the face: fear, rejection, inadequacy. But one day during a conversation, she shared her life story, and I was able to share mine—including how I came to Christ. I stepped over the barriers in my own heart and mind to sow gospel seeds that day.

My neighbor has not yet chosen to follow Jesus. Our families continue to be friends to this day—and I continue to pray that those seeds will be watered and take root.

In the salvation process, God's people are either tilling the soil, casting gospel seeds into the soil, watering the gospel seeds, or harvesting. The triune God is responsible for the results—not us. Just as a farmer cannot make it rain, we cannot make people believe in Jesus. God the Holy Spirit draws people to Jesus and opens their eyes to see their need for him. Some people resist and reject God's offer of salvation.[1] Some people believe.[2]

When we get stuck on the results (or lack thereof), we can create all sorts of internal barriers that keep us from sharing our faith. And that's completely normal! I'd venture to guess that very few of us feel utterly confident in sharing our faith.

How do we overcome those barriers? We can pay attention to the ways we might struggle to do our part in God's gospel work. To be everyday missionaries, we need to take a hard look at ourselves and what keeps us from letting God's love overflow out of us and into the people around us.

Barriers = Opportunities

If sharing the gospel with other people is meant to be a way of life for a disciple of Jesus, why do most of us *not* share our faith? Lifeway Research offers some insight from their study of unchurched Americans:

> Despite the openness and relationships with Christians, few unchurched Americans have ever had someone explain exactly how to become a Christian or why they should think about doing so. Only 3 in 10 unchurched Americans (29%) say a Christian has ever shared with them one-on-one how a person becomes a Christian.[3]

What keeps us from doing this? Theologian Ken Boa suggests that most followers of Jesus do not share their faith because of six common barriers:[4]

The Barrier of Method
The Barrier of Fear
The Barrier of Inadequacy
The Barrier of Indifference
The Barrier of Shame
The Barrier of Time

Before I talk about these six barriers, let's adjust our mindset. These barriers aren't walls; they're invitations. *When you're lit up with love, you know that barriers are opportunities to press deeper into Christ and rely on the Holy Spirit's power.* When you choose to let God walk with you past the barriers, three things will happen:

- You will fall deeper in love with Jesus because you will discover how good it is to rest in his indwelling presence.[5]
- You will be sensitive to God's missional heart to reach the lost.
- Your confidence as an everyday missionary will flourish. Instead of trying to do God's job, you will let him do his job through you.[6]

The Barrier of Method

Evangelism, which is sharing the gospel, is often associated with high-pressure sales techniques, and that's an understandable barrier for a lot of us when it comes to sharing our faith. Jesus isn't a product we're selling, and people shouldn't feel pressured or like we're just trying to "close the deal." Here are a few *unhelpful* methods of sharing Jesus with the lost that turn even Christians away from conversations about faith:

- *The Flame Thrower.* This person is on a college campus or downtown in a city near you. They are experts at spewing hate at people who don't know God. Instead of offering friendship to sinners like Jesus did, these misguided people are offering condemnation.

- *The Big-Game Hunter.* This person is looking for the next head (convert) they can place on their trophy wall. They are not driven by the love of Christ; they are driven by ego.

- *The Awkward Guy.* This person doesn't read the room—they barrel forth like an unbroken horse into conversations about Jesus. In my early years of following Jesus, I was this guy. I had so much zeal but not the spiritual maturity to connect well with people and share the gospel. I was moving in my own strength, not the Holy Spirit's—which made me awkward when sharing Jesus. (Remarkably, people still came to faith in Christ!)

- *The Faker.* This person knowingly waters down the gospel to make it appealing to the lost. They present Jesus as a self-help coach. Instead of sharing how Jesus overthrew sin, death, and evil, they make him sound like a divine butler.

- *The Body Slammer.* This person puts an intense amount of pressure on people to follow Jesus. Once a pastor told me he led a man to Christ while in a public bathroom. I found myself thinking, *He probably said yes so he could use the restroom in peace!*

Yes, Scripture tells us that the gospel is offensive—but our approach to sharing it doesn't have to be.[7] Sadly, we as followers of Jesus can become offensive in how we talk to people who don't know him—bringing judgment or condescension, or treating them like a box to check on our Jesus-follower to-do list. The gospel is offensive because *grace* is offensive: The fact is, we are sinners in need of a Savior, and there is nothing we can do to save ourselves. When I first heard that I was a sinner in need of a Savior, I was offended. Like most people do, I said, "I'm a good person." Only when the Holy Spirit gave me eyes to see that only God is good and that everyone has sinned did I become aware of my need for Jesus.

As everyday missionaries, we shouldn't be offensive in how we communicate the greatest news ever: There is a life-giving, sin-forgiving, righteous-making Savior named Jesus. He is the Lord of the universe. And through faith in him, you can be rescued from darkness and brought into his marvelous light!

The Barrier of Fear

The biggest barrier to sharing our faith is fear.

We are afraid of being rejected.

We're afraid of failing.

We are afraid of being branded "weird."

We're afraid of offending someone.

Fear paralyzes us from reaching people who don't know Jesus. Our fear of sharing the Good News is really about us focusing too much on ourselves. Instead of being absorbed in Jesus, we are absorbed in our own reputation, our self-image, the perception people have of us. But when we focus on Jesus, his perfect love overcomes fear.[8]

When people reject the gospel, they are rejecting Jesus, not us. It's not our gospel. Whatever people decide to do with what we share is between them and Jesus. We are simply messengers commanded to love our neighbor as we love ourselves.

Our fear of sharing the gospel is also rooted in an insufficient view of God.[9] We don't trust God's power and work in people's lives, so we subconsciously believe that we are the ones in control of what happens. But we are not God the Holy Spirit. We can't save anyone. Paul says, "No one can say, 'Jesus is Lord,' except by the Holy Spirit."[10] He does *not* say, "No can say, 'Jesus is Lord,' except by Derwin."

The power to save belongs to the triune God alone. When we choose to truly understand who God is and what he does, we can rest in knowing he is drawing people to himself.[11] Gospel seeds that I sow today may lay dormant in a person's heart for years before they sprout. God saves, and we can trust him to save his lost sheep!

When you're lit up with love, your fear becomes an opportunity— because you acknowledge the fear and let it push you deeper into relying on the Holy Spirit's power.[12] The strongest people in God's family are the weakest because they depend on his strength. Their confidence is rooted in the only One who conquered sin and death. They know that God "has not given us a spirit of fear and timidity, but of power, love, and self-discipline."[13] When fear tries to keep us silent, let's say the name of Jesus—because only he saves sinners.

The Barrier of Inadequacy

Most of the time when I share Jesus with the lost, I feel inadequate. I think, *What if they ask a question I don't know the answer to? What if they bring up a way Christians or Christian leaders have failed or hurt them?* If a person asks me a question that I do not know the answer to, I've learned to say, "I don't know. Why don't we study the topic together?" If someone becomes angry or combative, I say, "I'm sorry if I offended you. I can see this is a hard topic to discuss. Let's take a break. If you want to talk at another time, I'm more than willing." When someone asks me about a church scandal or shares about how Christians have hurt them, I apologize. I've learned to say, "What happened was evil and must never happen again. I stand with you against evil. Sadly, often Jesus' people act in ways that are the opposite of Jesus. But Jesus will never hurt you. He is the only sinless and safe person, and he will keep and sustain you."

When you think about sharing your faith with someone, do you feel inadequate too? Perhaps you play out scenarios in your mind where someone starts asking you theological questions you can't answer. Or maybe you envision accidentally saying the "wrong" thing, prompting them to become combative or angry.

I have some good news for both of us: God the Holy Spirit

uses inadequate people like you and me in mind-blowing, transformative ways!

> Such is the confidence we have through Christ before
> God. It is not that we are competent in ourselves to claim
> anything as coming from ourselves, but our adequacy is
> from God.
>
> 2 CORINTHIANS 3:4-5, CSB

This barrier of inadequacy is also an invitation. Jesus is calling you to grow in the grace and knowledge of knowing him. For example, if you're noticing that you are nervous about sharing some aspect of the gospel or being asked about some theological point, you don't have to stay in that feeling: You can do something with it.

When I first came to Jesus, I was enthusiastic with very little biblical knowledge. One day, I was sharing the gospel with someone who didn't know Jesus—but who did know the Bible. He turned me into a theological pretzel. After being spiritually kicked around like a soccer ball for two hours, I walked to my car with my head hanging low. Before I drove off, I put my head on the steering wheel and cried. Then I made Jesus a promise: that I would never allow that to happen again. I promised to study the Bible and learn theology and apologetics. Jesus has done too much for me and the world for me not to prepare myself for conversations about him.[14] One of the reasons I have a doctorate in the New Testament in context and a master of divinity with a concentration in apologetics is because of that moment. *When you're lit up with love, you want to be equipped for whatever questions or needs you encounter.*

But we don't need an advanced degree in theology or apologetics to study Scripture and learn how to thoughtfully respond to many people's most basic questions.[15] While we don't need to be counselors or pastors to empathize with how they've been wounded, Jesus is too good and too beautiful for us not to study and be prepared.[16] He is too invested in people's restoration for us to not learn how to be with them in their pain.

The Barrier of Indifference

Sadly, many of Jesus' people are indifferent toward sharing the gospel with the lost. *Indifference* means that a person is unsympathetic, unconcerned, or lacks interest in something. Why does this happen with something as important as the gospel?

My conviction is that if we do not feel like it matters for us to share the gospel, we have lost our first love.[17] If we are not intentional about remaining connected to Jesus, our light of love will grow dim under "the worries of this age, the deceitfulness of wealth, and the desires for other things [that] enter in and choke the word, and it becomes unfruitful."[18] Instead of worshiping Jesus and abiding in him, we start to worship the things God gives us: our jobs, our money, our kids, our status. When we become self-centered instead of Christ centered, we go through life asking Jesus to bless our agendas instead of joining Jesus in his agenda of restoring people to God.

But all is not lost. Our relationship with Jesus must be—and *can be*—cultivated. Just as quality time and regular conversation in a marriage breathes life into that relationship, the Holy Spirit will connect our hearts more deeply to Jesus' heart as we soak in the Scriptures, live lives of prayer, set our minds on Christ, and participate in corporate worship.[19]

We are also often indifferent because we no longer see the world's deep need. The longer most people follow Jesus, the fewer non-Christian friends they have. Often new believers are the most passionate about sharing their faith because they still have lots of friends who are lost. But as they participate in the church more, they increasingly hang around other Christians.

The church should be a missionary-training center, not a country club for the saved. As a pastor, I am supposed to partner with God the Holy Spirit in activating believers to reach those who don't know Jesus; as a follower of Jesus, I should ensure my time with other Christians encourages and equips me to be in relationships with the lost.[20] *When you're lit up with love, you know that the stakes are too high for you to be indifferent.*[21]

The Barrier of Shame

Early in my faith walk with Jesus, the barrier of shame prevented me from sharing my faith, especially with people who knew me before I followed Jesus. I would think, *How can I talk about Jesus when three weeks ago I was partying with this guy?* Or if I ran into someone I hadn't seen since before I knew Jesus, I would think, *I can't share Christ—they knew the old me.* The voices in my head were lies from the dark powers who didn't want me to share Christ. But grace is for people who have a past—like me!

The barrier of shame has become an increasingly significant roadblock to sharing the gospel due to cultural pressures, particularly in certain places in America and Europe. Some of us are ashamed of how some of our siblings in Christ speak and behave. Some of us are ashamed of certain historic doctrinal beliefs that Christians have guarded for two millennia. Some of us are ashamed of how Christians have treated people in the LGBTQ+ community.[22] Some of us are ashamed of the ways Christianity is sometimes publicly associated with ungodliness like racism or abuse.

Many of these points of shame should indeed cause us to grieve.[23] We should grieve how our own brokenness and sin, even within the church, has harmed others. But as with many other barriers, when we let this grief become shame, we make it about us, not about God and his message. The Good News of Jesus' reconciling salvation isn't something to be ashamed of. We're not inviting people into an institution—we're inviting people into a relationship. *When you're lit up with love, you don't let the power of shame silence you; instead, you let the power of God amplify your voice.*

Once a person who was exploring a relationship with Jesus said to me, "Derwin, throughout history, people who have identified as Christians have done horrible things!" They were shocked when I agreed. "Yes," I said, "some people who say they follow Jesus have done some ugly, ungodly things. Some have done some beautiful, godly things. Ultimately, your salvation is not in people. Your salvation is in Jesus alone." I am a Christian because Jesus died and rose again. He loves me. He lives in me. He has always been faithful and good to me. I could never be ashamed of Jesus. He was not ashamed of me and my sin when he died so I could live. He boldly and beautifully went to the cross for me. By his grace and his power, I will boldly and (I hope) beautifully go into the world proclaiming his rescuing love.

> I am not ashamed of this Good News about Christ. It is the power of God at work, saving everyone who believes—the Jew first and also the Gentile. This Good News tells us how God makes us right in his sight. This is accomplished from start to finish by faith. As the Scriptures say, "It is through faith that a righteous person has life."
>
> ROMANS 1:16-17

The Barrier of Time

Many of us feel we barely have the energy or margin to get through our busy days, much less prioritize relationships and conversations with people who don't know Jesus. I've heard it said that "BUSY is an acronym for Being Under Satan's Yoke." Our modern age is designed to make us busy and tired. As one writer warns:

> Being busy is not a badge of honor and we must reverse this dangerous cultural phenomenon by resisting the urge to brag about how busy we are. The busy brag is pervasive.[24]

But we are not doomed to an endlessly busy life. We can choose to slow down, to be more present to Jesus, ourselves, and other people. When we prioritize Jesus and his Kingdom, we increasingly find our time shaped by what matters most. We notice what is unnecessary—what has to do with our pressures rather than God's priorities—and we begin to cut out those things. For example, I've chosen to limit my time on social media. I'm happier. I have less anxiety. I'm more present to my wife and children. And I have more time to read and engage with lost people.

If being worn down by busyness is sabotaging you from joining Jesus on mission, I encourage you to choose the opportunity to slow down. What would it look like if you let Jesus shape your priorities? I have found that the more I immerse myself in Jesus through prayer, Scripture meditation, and study and the more time I spend in community with other followers of Jesus, the more my life aligns with Jesus' heart. *When you're lit up with love, you align your life with Jesus' priorities so you can see where he is working and have the energy to join him.* One day the Lord will ask us, "What did you do with the precious time I gave you on earth?" May we say, "Lord, we followed you. And you led us to your lost sheep."

Barriers like method, fear, inadequacy, indifference, shame, and time will always tempt us to stay silent rather than engage with people who don't know Jesus. But we can choose to see those barriers and turn them into opportunities to look to Christ, call out to Christ, and trust in the power of Christ. And when we do, the perfect love of Jesus will shine through the darkness of shame and cast out all fear.[25]

Barriers to sharing the gospel will always be present. The dark powers of evil do not want lost people to be found. However, just like the stone that enclosed the tomb of Christ was rolled away by the love of God, barriers to sharing our faith will be rolled away by the God who lights his people up with love.

Holy Habits

- *When you're lit up with love, you know that barriers are opportunities to press deeper into Christ and rely on the Holy Spirit's power.*

- *When you're lit up with love, your fear becomes an opportunity— because you acknowledge the fear and let it push you deeper into relying on the Holy Spirit's power.*

- *When you're lit up with love, you want to be equipped for whatever questions or needs you encounter.*

- *When you're lit up with love, you know that the stakes are too high for you to be indifferent.*

- *When you're lit up with love, you don't let the power of shame silence you; instead, you let the power of God amplify your voice.*

- *When you're lit up with love, you align your life with Jesus' priorities so you can see where he is working and have the energy to join him.*

Reflection Questions

1. Have you encountered or observed any of the unhelpful methods of sharing Jesus described here? What was the result? How is what we talk about in this book different from those approaches?

2. What are some ways you sense you could grow in your ability to answer people's deepest questions about God? What are some steps you could take toward that this week?

3. Do you have many (or any) friends who are not Christians? If not, where could you start cultivating friendships so you encounter the world's deep need more regularly?

4. Which of the six internal barriers to sharing your faith do you struggle the most with? How could you turn that barrier into an opportunity?

PRAYER

Father, Son, and Holy Spirit,

Change my mindset.

May I see barriers to sharing my faith

as opportunities to share my faith.

You love to work through people who rely on you.

Today I commit to relying on you

to reach people you love with the gospel.

I am yours.

Send me.

I'll go.

In Jesus' name, amen.

CHAPTER 9

REMOVE EVERY OBSTACLE

Facing the World's Resistance to the Gospel

When my children were in elementary school, I would read to their classes. I wanted my kids to know that their dad was there for them and that I loved them. A few years ago, I ran into one of their now-grown classmates, who was working at a restaurant I like, and we began talking. This young man told me he was spiritual and did not know much about the Bible but that he believed he was connected with the universe and could manifest his own destiny. Over the course of several conversations, I shared the gospel with him. He listened, but he was not receptive.

But then, a few years later, I saw him at Transformation Church. He told me, "Pastor, I follow Jesus now."

I asked, "What happened?"

He said, "Jesus sent Christians like you who loved me, shared the gospel, and answered my questions."

Many of the barriers to sharing our faith are internal, but just as many involve other human beings: the people we interact with in a post-Christian reality. Globally, Christianity is expanding (particularly in the Global South), often amid persecution and resistance, but Christianity in America is in decline. While America was never a "Christian nation," born-again followers of Jesus have always been a significant part of the American story. But now, America, like Europe before us, is entering a post-Christian reality. The Christian story of redemption through Christ is no longer the framing story of our society (and neither is Christian ethics). Many people don't know Bible stories, let alone Jesus' gospel.

Pastor and apologist Tim Keller, who planted Redeemer Presbyterian Church in post-Christian New York City in 1989, provides great insight to our current moment:

> In a society like ours, most people only know of either a very mild, nominal Christianity or a separatist, legalistic Christianity. Neither of these is, may we say, "the real thing." But exposure to them creates spiritual antibodies, as it were, making the listener extremely resistant to the gospel. These antibodies are now everywhere in our society.[1]

As everyday missionaries, even when we overcome our own barriers to sharing the gospel, cultural and spiritually we are surrounded by the reality that people in our world are predisposed to resist God's Good News.[2] That doesn't mean they aren't spiritually open though.[3] We have the honor of living out of the truth that God is on the move in people's hearts while we lean into the reality that God alone rescues people. The triune God doesn't need our *ability* to save; he just wants our *availability* to love and share.

How do I know that? Because we've been here before. The first-century Greco-Roman world in which Jesus, the apostle Paul, and the first followers of Jesus lived was very much like twenty-first-century America. And how the first Christians lived and shared the gospel provides a road map for moving through the barriers we face today.[4] God worked through obstacles then. He will do it again.

The Barrier of Pluralism

Just like twenty-first-century America, the first-century Greco-Roman world was filled with and shaped by religious pluralism. *Religious pluralism* means that in a religiously diverse society, individuals have the freedom to choose what (and whether) they want to believe. In the first century, people could follow any number of ancient philosophies and religions (as long as their particular beliefs didn't cause too much trouble for Rome). We see this when the apostle Paul was in Athens: He was overwhelmed by the sheer number of gods the Athenians worshiped.[5] As W. J. Conybeare and J. S. Howson observe in *The Life and Epistles of St. Paul*:

> There were more gods in Athens than in all the rest of the country, and the Roman satirist hardly exaggerates when he says that it was easier to find a god there than a man.[6]

We might not term our modern-day American pluralism "religious," but the reality is that we have lots of gods we turn to for identity, help, comfort, and hope. We worship things like money; sex; political power; alcohol; drugs; national superiority; our ethnicities; sports; various world religions; and nominal Christianity, which gives a false sense of identity, hope, and religious dedication without the heart change and life change of actually knowing Jesus.

America was founded on religious freedom and religious pluralism: People are free to choose which religion they want to follow. Since we live in a land with so many spiritual options, what can we learn from the early church about being everyday missionaries in a pluralistic society?

First, it's vital that we embrace the reality that Jesus will share his glory with no one; therefore, in a pluralistic society, we can expect pushback to Jesus' all-encompassing truth claims of salvation in him alone. If Jesus is Lord, as everyday missionaries, we are commanded to worship him alone and to reach those whom he longs to grip with his saving grace. We believe humanity is on a sinking ship, and we are called by

Jesus to jump into the rough seas and rescue drowning people. Jesus, the apostle Paul, and the early church got in trouble with the Roman Empire because Rome's posture was essentially this: Worship whatever you want—as long as you acknowledge Caesar as Lord and your primary allegiance is to Rome. Jesus was crucified for acting like he was "King of the Jews"[7] and declaring that he was the one true God.[8] In Thessalonica, the apostle Paul was charged with turning "the world upside down" because he was "saying that there is another king—Jesus."[9] The early church experienced persecution under madmen like Roman emperor Domitian, who demanded that he be addressed as "lord and god."[10] No matter the cost, though, the men and women in the early church remained *lit up with love: They continued to worship Jesus alone, putting him before every idol*—even those things that can become idols today, like nationalism, ethnic pride, and political affiliation.

What cultural expectations does our faith conflict with now? In a pluralistic society like America, we can believe whatever we want, as long as we don't say that Jesus is the only way to salvation. We can live what we believe, as long as our beliefs don't confront political hot topics or call out racial injustice or sexual immorality. But a Christianity where God is only personal and not someone we can talk about or introduce other people to is incomplete, lacking the love-fueled, life-transforming power human beings are truly longing for. *When you're lit up with love, you know that reaching lost people with the gospel is a matter of life and death.*

According to the apostle Paul, behind every idol is a demon,[11] and those dark powers of evil have one goal: to "steal and kill and destroy" us.[12] The dark powers seduce human beings away from the God who loves them with the same old lie: You can save yourself, prove yourself, fix yourself, make yourself good enough to be accepted by God or live a happy life or become the person you want to be. Pluralism expects us to be content for the people around us to die in that lie.

Amid this world of religious pluralism stands bloodstained Jesus, proclaiming, "I am the way and the truth and the life. No one comes to the Father except through me."[13] We cannot save ourselves. Salvation can't be found in any other name.[14] *When you're lit up with love, you join Jesus in proclaiming that he is the Way, the Truth, and the Life and that no one comes to the Father except through him.* The Holy Spirit opens our eyes and moves us to actively look for people who have realized that no idol can fill the longing within them. No false god can offer the forgiveness, freedom, and fellowship that only Jesus gives. When idols fail, we can point people to Jesus.

The Barrier of Political Idolatry

While it may feel like the political polarization of our day is worse than it's ever been, people in the first century looked to political leaders for peace, prosperity, and security just like so many do in twenty-first-century America. N. T. Wright says,

> Everybody else [but the Jews] in Saul's [Paul's] day, in regions from Spain to Syria, had to worship the goddess Roma and *Kyrios Caesar*, "Lord Caesar." Augustus Caesar declared that his late adoptive father, Julius Caesar, was now divine, thus conveniently acquiring for himself the title *divi filius*, "son of the deified one," or in Greek simply *huios theou*, "son of god." His successors mostly followed suit. The cults of Roma and the emperor spread.[15]

We may not think of our modern political allegiances as idolatry, but too often the reality is that even (and sometimes especially) Christians conflate dependence on God with reliance on political positions, candidates, or judicial decisions. As a result, people who don't know God often think they must align with one political party or another to follow Jesus.

Political idolatry hurts evangelism not only because it isn't about drawing people to the one true God but also because it's dividing the church. When we allow the clouded chaos of the kingdom of man to enter the picture, the love-lit invitation to the Kingdom of God dims.

Salvation is by grace through faith in Christ. No political affiliation adds to or takes away from the power of grace. In the two thousand years since Jesus started his church, most of his followers have never heard of a Republican or Democrat. Even today, American Christians comprise only a fraction of the global church. A recent study on global Christianity made encouraging projections for the growth of Christianity and the distribution of Christians by 2050:[16]

REGION	PROJECTED NUMBER OF CHRISTIANS BY 2050 (IN MILLIONS)
Africa	1,282
Latin America	679
Asia	585
Europe	489
North America	258
Oceania	33

That doesn't mean we absent ourselves from engaging with our nation's political process or from seeking "the peace and prosperity of the city" in which we are exiles.[17] Believers should vote their conscience, standing up for justice and embodying love. But our first priority should always be the heart of Jesus. We must not let any worldly thing distract us from joining Jesus on his mission of reaching lost people with the gospel.

The Barrier of Partiality

In the first-century Greco-Roman world, it was common for some Greeks to look down on anyone who wasn't Greek.[18] Bible commentator William Barclay explained it this way: "The Greeks called anyone who could not speak Greek a barbarian; and they despised such people and put up the barriers against them."[19] Some Jews of that day would thank God for not making them a Gentile, a woman, or a slave.[20] The apostle Peter acknowledged this attitude when he said, "You are well aware that it is against our law for a Jew to associate with or visit a Gentile. But God has shown me that I should not call anyone impure or unclean."[21]

If ethnocentrism, classism, and sexism were problems in the world of the early church, we shouldn't be surprised that these remain significant barriers today. Sadly, Christian history is far from exempt: Christians have used the name of Jesus to participate in racism, sexism, and classism. This is an evil malpractice of the gospel that hurts the message of Christ! If we want to reach future generations, we must tell the story of how the Cross of Jesus has crucified the sins of ethnocentrism, classism, and sexism.

When we as Jesus' church are following our calling, we offer a new vision for human community where ethnic diversity is not obliterated but celebrated.[22] Men and women are coheirs and coequals in Christ. The rich, the poor, and the middle class are all equal and one in Christ.[23] In a fractured, postmodern world, the gospel creates and invites people into a multiethnic, multigenerational family where men and women, rich and poor love one another and work side by side for the sake of the Kingdom. What would people who don't know Jesus think if they saw the unity of God's people lived out? Wouldn't that be a bright light of good news?

The Intellectual, Emotional, and Volitional Barriers

Some people struggle with belief in Jesus because they have *intellectual* barriers. Some people are working through *emotional* barriers because they, or people they know, have experienced suffering or been hurt by someone who follows Jesus. And some people don't want to follow Jesus because he demands they surrender their sins at the foot of the Cross. This is called the *volitional* barrier.

Each of these barriers offers us opportunities to meet people where they are. It's a sacred privilege to journey with people as they seek answers to their questions. Our faith is reasonable. This is why understanding Christian apologetics is so important when we are speaking to people who don't know Jesus.

When people have emotional barriers to faith in Christ, we must approach them with patience and compassion. Be with them in their hurt; don't try to explain away or excuse their pain. But also don't be afraid to point people to Jesus. Jesus has never hurt them. Jesus will never hurt them. Jesus is the only safe person, our only place of lasting refuge. When an orchestra misplays Beethoven, we don't blame Beethoven—we blame the orchestra. When people misrepresent Jesus through word or action, we don't blame Jesus—we hold his followers accountable. This is why we must point people to Jesus, not to ourselves or any other person.

Last, when people are struggling with a volitional barrier, we must stay present and prayerful. We cannot change hearts, nor should we try to. In fact, we become a barrier to God's work in a person's life when we decide it's our responsibility to argue them out of their sin and into salvation. Our role is to love them and be ready for the moments when God's pursuit breaks through their resistance.

Each of these barriers presents an opportunity to love, to pray for, and to be present in the lives of people who are exploring the claims of Jesus. You can be a thoughtful space for their intellectual questions, a compassionate person in their emotional struggles, and a steady presence of grace despite their volitional barriers. You are an everyday missionary: called by God, indwelt by the Son, and empowered by the Holy Spirit. God can and will minister through you to change people's earthly time and eternal destinies.

Think and Act like Missionaries

Often high school football players will ask me how I developed the confidence it takes to play in the NFL. I tell them that confidence is spelled *p-r-e-p-a-r-a-t-i-o-n*. We grow in confidence over time as we prepare for a task. For example, a player develops the confidence to play in the NFL through years of doing tough, consistent offseason training; studying games; practicing like they are playing in the game; learning to trust teammates and coaches; choosing proper nutrition; investing in body recovery; and prioritizing quality sleep. When the game finally happens, you have faith in your preparation.

A person doesn't rise to the level of the moment. They rise to the level of their preparation. The most authentically confident people are the most prepared people. The most confident everyday missionaries are those who know and live the gospel, soak in Scripture, rely on the Holy Spirit, and rehearse in their minds potential conversations they may have about the gospel. *When you're lit up with love, you think and act like a missionary because you are a missionary.*

I find that learning from the apostle Paul helps me prepare for engaging faithfully in a culture skeptical of the gospel. First, Paul was fueled by worship. The greater our worship of Jesus, the greater our passion will be for others to worship him.[24] *Worship is the fuel for mission.* Paul's worship led him on mission to reach the world. Second, in his visit to Mars Hill in Athens, Paul embodied seven missional traits that show us how to be effective in Good-Newsing lost people—no matter the barrier:

1. *Paul was distressed over the idolatry in Athens.*[25] Athens was full of idols, and Paul knew that behind every idol is a demon. He had a holy burden for the people of Athens. The first step in cultivating a missional heart in a lost world is to recognize the needs of lost people. When you have a love for lost people, a missional heart will give you the courage to share your faith, regardless of the barrier. Ask God to give you a burden for the lost, and he will.

2. *Paul engaged in cross-cultural, multiethnic evangelism.*[26] Paul shared the gospel with Jews and Gentiles. He wanted everyone saved—included in God's family—regardless of their ethnicity. As a Jew, he knew God promised Abraham a multiethnic family. Jesus is the seed of Abraham who creates this family through his life, death, and resurrection.[27] Jesus desires to save every person, and Scripture tells us that one day every nation, every tribe, and every tongue will worship him. Jesus' passion fuels us to reach lost people across cultural and ethnic lines.[28] God's heart for being reconciled to humanity gives us a heart for racial reconciliation. The local church is a community on earth where racism and prejudice should not exist because all God's children are clothed in Christ and are one in Christ.[29]

3. *Paul was curious about people who didn't know Jesus.* He frequently spent time in Jewish synagogues and in Gentile marketplaces. Everyday missionaries are curious about people. We want to discover their stories, their hopes, and their pain. My Gen Z son, Jeremiah, does this beautifully. Because he loves Jesus, he loves lost people. And because he loves lost people, he is genuinely curious about them. Over the years, I have watched people open their souls to him. Many people

have come to faith in Jesus because of his gentle, loving presence. As he learns their stories, he applies the saving action of Jesus to their wounds. *When you're lit up with love, you learn how to listen well so you can share the gospel in a way that connects with the stories of those around you.*

4. *Paul found common ground with the lost.*[30] Missionaries meet people where they are so they can take them to Jesus. Paul saw that the Athenians worshiped many gods—they even had an altar to an unknown one! This gave him the common ground he was seeking to establish. He told them who the unknown God was. In our post-Christian culture, people are spiritually open, which means that while conversations about Christianity can be a barrier for some, common ground is an entry point.

Once, after a gentleman shared his version of the philosophy of karma with me, I said, "We all need a do-over in life, don't we? We long for a way to make up for wrongs we've done. The problem with karma is that your present life is the result of your past life. How do you know when you lived a good enough life to improve your outcome in the next life? Or worse, what if this life makes your next life one of suffering?"

Then I told him, "This is why I am so grateful for grace. The grace of Jesus wipes my slate clean, forgives and forgets my sin, gives me power to align my life to his life, and assures me I'll be brought to new life in a new heaven and new earth." He found what I said compelling and wanted to talk further.

Find common ground. Then walk together toward the Cross.

5. *Paul pointed people to the God of Scripture.* Paul described the unknown God[31] on Mars Hill as the Creator, Sustainer, Ruler, Father, and Judge.[32] John Stott says,

> People are looking for an integrated world-view which makes sense of all their experience. We learn from Paul that we cannot preach the gospel of Jesus without the doctrine of God, or the cross without the creation, or salvation without judgment. Today's world needs a bigger gospel, the full gospel of Scripture.[33]

In our post-Christian culture, people are curious about who God is, what God has done, and how knowing God can transform their lives. A world that doesn't know about God needs to see a robust, beautiful picture of the Father, the Son, and the Holy Spirit. In my experience, the more I share that the living Creator is all-loving, all-powerful, and all-knowing, and that he desires to know and love people, the more curious people become. Lost people are not looking for a puny, watered-down version of God. Give them the big, beautiful, life-giving God of Scripture revealed in King Jesus.

6. *Paul called the Athenians to repentance.*[34] Repentance means turning from idols and turning to Jesus for the forgiveness of sins. The "unknown god" can be known: His name is Jesus, the One who rose from the dead and wants everyone to repent and give their lives to him.[35] The Holy Spirit is working on people when you share the gospel with them. You do not have to manipulate or pressure them. Just love them and share the gospel. As the Spirit moves on them, you can call them to repentance and faith in Jesus.

7. *Paul trusted in God's sovereignty for results.* When Paul finished his two-minute speech on Mars Hill, some ridiculed him, some agreed to hear him more, and some believed, "including Dionysius the Areopagite, a woman named Damaris, and others with them."[36] It's God's job to save. It's our job to love people and cast gospel seeds into souls.

For Such a Time as This

It's no accident that you are alive at this time in the history of the world. Our loving God, in his sovereign genius, has called you by grace and equipped you with the Spirit to be an everyday missionary right where you are, to the people you interact with in our post-Christian culture. A life spent with Jesus is a life on mission with him. The barriers we face are opportunities to draw on the infinite, eternal, all-powerful resources of Jesus. This is worship. For such a time as this, you get to become a Good-News person in our gospel-starved world.

Think like a missionary.

Act like a missionary.

Because *you are* a missionary.

And you have the Good News that the world needs.

And this is what God has testified: He has given us eternal life, and this life is in his Son. Whoever has the Son has life; whoever does not have God's Son does not have life.

I have written this to you who believe in the name of the Son of God, so that you may know you have eternal life.

1 JOHN 5:11-13

Holy Habits

- *When you're lit up with love, you worship Jesus alone, putting him before every idol.*

- *When you're lit up with love, you know that reaching lost people with the gospel is a matter of life and death.*

- *When you're lit up with love, you join Jesus in proclaiming that he is the Way, the Truth, and the Life and that no one comes to the Father except through him.*

- *When you're lit up with love, you think and act like a missionary because you are a missionary.*

- *When you're lit up with love, you learn how to listen well so you can share the gospel in a way that connects with the stories of those around you.*

Reflection Questions

1. What is a post-Christian culture? How do you notice ours in your everyday contexts? Why is understanding the post-Christian nature of our culture important?

2. What barriers will you face in a post-Christian culture? Have you encountered them in your community, workplace, or other regular contexts?

3. Which barrier is the most daunting to you? How can you overcome it?

4. Reflect on the seven missional traits of an everyday missionary. Which is the most energizing to you, and why?

PRAYER

Father,

In our post-Christian culture,

would you give me a heart like yours

for people who do not know your Son, Jesus?

King Jesus,

You came to seek and save the lost.

Give me a heart like yours for the lost.

Holy Spirit,

Enable me to think and act like a missionary.

May the holy flame of God's love ignite my heart

and equip me to introduce people to Jesus.

Amen.

CHAPTER 10

OPEN YOUR EYES

Lighting Up a Dark World

For nearly thirty years, I've watched my wife, Vicki, lead people to Christ. And what stands out to me every time is her dependence on the Holy Spirit. She is Spirit-filled in how she prays for people, how she loves people, how she is patient with people, and how her life makes people curious about Jesus.

Vicki pays attention to the Spirit's timing and trusts that he'll show her when a person's heart is soft toward Jesus. Once, Vicki told me how she longed for deeper conversations, conversations about things that mattered, with one of our neighbors. She had spent years sharing Christ with this woman, yet the conversations seemed to be going nowhere. But she listened to the Spirit, and she didn't force things. She could sense that this woman was not ready in that particular season of life. But when our neighbor's dad got sick and eventually passed away, Vicki was right by her side. All those gospel seeds took root and blossomed: This neighbor came to Christ and, for years now, has gone on medical mission trips around the world sharing the gospel.

The God who forgives sins and raises the dead is not looking for superheroes. He's looking for people who are *super dependent* on the Holy Spirit—people who are ready to listen to his voice and follow his lead so others can know him.

Just as the Father sent the Son into the world, God is sending you to be an everyday missionary, bringing his love into and through your network of relationships. When we are lit up with love, we become a *missional* people who show up in distinct ways in our communities and relationships: with missional imagination, missional presence, missional relationship, and missional action.

Missional Imagination

One of the greatest gifts God gives us is our imaginations. Part of how we develop the heart and motivation to reach other people with the Good News is by *cultivating a missional imagination* for what God might be up to and how he may want to express himself through us right where we are. We do this by soaking in Scripture: reading it, praying it, speaking it, and living it in Christian community. We cultivate a Christ-centered understanding of the Bible, knowing that all of it points to him and his redemptive mission that conquered sin and death and reconciled humanity and creation to himself.[1] As we practice our missional imagination, the Holy Spirit gives us creative ideas for how we can be available to share the gospel in our daily lives.

In my early days of pastoring, I began to notice that when pastors or ministry leaders got into "ministry," they spent less and less time around people who didn't know Jesus. There was no way I wanted to limit sharing the greatest news in the world to only preaching on Sunday—but I also knew that I was going to have to make intentional choices to make sure conversations with people outside the church were part of my everyday life.

I asked God to form me into an everyday missionary, and as I prayed, I sensed that I needed to do my studying at a coffee shop near my house. Over the years, I have had hundreds of gospel conversations there. Multiple people have come to faith in Jesus. Recently, one of those people was baptized at Transformation Church. As she walked into the baptismal pool, we locked eyes, and both of us smiled.

Using your *missional imagination* in the Spirit's power is a holy habit we can all practice. *Sometimes your best ability is your availability.* Ask God to help you envision how and where you can bring his light into your context. He will answer that prayer!

Missional Presence

Vino, a member of Transformation Church who now serves on our staff, was not always a follower of Jesus. As an upper-middle-class Hindu Indian woman, she would have never imagined herself following Jesus or being on a church staff. But today she is a growing disciple of Jesus because Jesus drew her to himself through the *missional presence* of an everyday missionary.

When a follower of Jesus is living out God's *missional presence*, they are drawing life from Jesus; relying on the Spirit's power; and walking prayerfully in compassion, humility, and love. No matter where they find themselves, a person with missional presence is aware that they are on mission with Jesus.[2] Those they meet sense that there is something different about them.

Vino met a follower of Jesus who lived out her faith. The *missional presence* of this woman was too compelling to ignore. As their relationship matured, the woman shared the gospel with Vino. Vino didn't like the idea of being a sinner, even though deep down she knew she was. Every human being, no matter our culture or context, can sense the gaping loss of not knowing the living God—even if they do not know that is what they are feeling.[3] The woman invited Vino to a Bible study with other followers of Jesus, where Vino learned about Jesus through the pages of Scripture. Vino says,

> Three months into [the] study of John's Gospel, I felt
> truly convicted and saw the need for Christ. No questions,

no arguments—I could feel his presence and believed that
he died for me on the cross. On sharing day, I professed
my faith to a group of ladies. I knew and believed God
loved me. I started doing BSF [Bible Study Fellowship]
and continue to this very day.

Missional presence means we lead with being *present with* people
who don't know Jesus and *present to* what God might be up to in their
lives. We do not lead with requirements of what someone must do or
change. Instead, we invite them into belonging before they believe.
Vino *belonged* to a Christian community before she believed what
Christians believed. *When you're lit up with love, you understand that
belonging often precedes believing.*

Cultivating a missional presence is vital because often the biggest
stumbling block to people coming to Jesus is not Jesus but us, his
people. When believers allow the things of this world to choke out
the gracious work of the Holy Spirit, we injure the cause of Christ.
*When you're lit up with love, you understand that your own discipleship
and transformation are priorities.* As followers of Jesus grow in their
faith, a discernible happiness and beautiful purposefulness emanate
from them like a life-giving perfume.[4]

Vino experienced God's presence through God's Word and in
the community of God's people. The Holy Spirit operated on Vino's
heart, cleaning the clogs out of her spiritual arteries, freeing the blood
of Jesus to circulate in her soul. She received Jesus as her Savior and
was baptized, symbolizing her entrance into God's multiethnic family
and allegiance to him.

Just as the precious woman who shared the gospel with Vino was a
missional presence in Vino's life, you are called to be the same in others'
lives. The Holy Spirit's power—through the missional presence of his
people and the proclamation of the gospel—is what leads people to

faith. Everyday missionaries are the *missional presence* of God in the world.

Missional Relationship

I love people because Jesus loves people. Every person who exists is precious and valuable—which means that every person I meet is worthy of dignity, love, and respect. Missional relationships equip us to see every lost person as Jesus sees them—not as a project or a problem but as a prodigal far from their Father's home. We connect with them, care about them, and get to know who they are and what matters to them. Our missional presence becomes more intentional: Not only does someone belong, but we invite them to be known and to know us in return.

In an angry world like ours, kindness goes a long way. When Jesus said, "Love your neighbor as yourself,"[5] he was demonstrating how the gospel empowers us to build missional relationships. We build missional relationships because people matter to us, and people matter to us because they matter to Jesus. When we're connected relationally with people who don't know Jesus, we're also connecting them with the body of Christ. We seek to be a blessing and to enrich others' lives because we're called to be holy conduits of God's love.

Missional relationships change lives because people are desperate to be truly loved. Sharing the Good News can't be about our agenda or ego—it must come from a place of deep, Cross-like love.[6] And just as love is expressed uniquely, so is sharing our faith. Here are some of the ways we can express the gospel:

- **Proclamation Evangelism:** The Lord may call you to the *proclamation* of the gospel, which happens in a preaching event like a church service or an evangelistic outreach. Think of Peter at Pentecost—his proclamation of the gospel helped lay the foundation of the early church.[7]

- **Confrontational Evangelism:** You may engage in *confrontational* evangelism by sharing the gospel with someone you have no relationship with. We see an example of this in the book of Acts when Philip struck up a conversation with the Ethiopian eunuch as they traveled along the same road.[8] Confrontational evangelism is not rude or intrusive. It's more about sensing the Holy Spirit calling you to share the gospel in the moment.

- **Missional Relationship:** Most followers of Jesus are primarily called to share their faith in quieter, more ordinary ways: through building relationships and investing time and presence with people in their spheres of influence. In the Holy Spirit's power, the love of Jesus goes out through everyday missionaries who work at their jobs with excellence and humility, who serve people well, who care for people compassionately, who cry with people when they mourn, and who live out peacemaking in a divisive world. When we as God's people prioritize blessing the lost, not only are we sharing the Good News—we become good news.[9]

Missional Action

As we grow in our missional imagination, discover how to be a missional presence in our context, and lean into missional relationships, we then move into two deliberate missional actions: prayer and care. Prayer connects our hearts to God's heart. And God's heart is for people to know and love his Son, the Light of the World. When I pray for people to know Jesus, I gain new eyes to see the brokenness in the world. Like the Good Samaritan,[10] we become people moved by love and compassion to offer God's sacrificial love to hurting people. The more we pray for people, the more we care for people.

Pray

We do not have the power to reach people on our own. *When you're lit up with love, you know that before you talk to people about Jesus, you must talk to Jesus about people.* I've discovered that the more I pray for the Holy Spirit to bring people who don't know him into my life, the more gospel-starved people show up around me.

As you engage lost people in conversations about Jesus, remember that the Holy Spirit opens their hearts, not us. *When you're lit up with love, you are burdened to see the lost found, and that holy burden moves you to prayer.* It is the Spirit's job to save. It is our sacred vocation to share the gospel in speech and actions. Prayer mysteriously puts us in positions to reach people with the gospel.

In my twenty-eight years of walking with Jesus, I have found that praying Scripture most quickly aligns me with God's heart for the lost. That's because, as Paul explained in his letter to Timothy, "Scripture is God-breathed."[11] When I pray passages like these, I am energized to reach out to the lost people Jesus wants to find:

> Jesus called out to them, "Come, follow me, and I will show you how to fish for people!"
> MATTHEW 4:19

> Jesus came and told his disciples, "I have been given all authority in heaven and on earth. Therefore, go and make disciples of all the nations, baptizing them in the name of the Father and the Son and the Holy Spirit. Teach these

new disciples to obey all the commands I have given you.
And be sure of this: I am with you always, even to the end
of the age."
MATTHEW 28:18-20

This is what God has testified: He has given us eternal
life, and this life is in his Son. Whoever has the Son
has life; whoever does not have God's Son does not
have life.

I have written this to you who believe in the name
of the Son of God, so that you may know you have
eternal life.
1 JOHN 5:11-13

God was in Christ, reconciling the world to himself,
no longer counting people's sins against them. And he
gave us this wonderful message of reconciliation. So
we are Christ's ambassadors; God is making his appeal
through us. We speak for Christ when we plead,
"Come back to God!"
2 CORINTHIANS 5:19-20

Care

People do not care what you have to say until they know you care
about them. Sharing Jesus is not a box to be checked off a to-do list but
an investment in a person of vast worth whom Jesus died to redeem.
Caring for people looks like journeying with them through their pains
and questions and triumphs and dreams. This is what I experienced
through the Naked Preacher and several other Indianapolis Colts
teammates who showed me Jesus' heart. They answered my questions,

prayed for me when I was injured, and were patient with me when I was not kind to them.

You can show up in people's lives with this kind of care too. You don't need to have all the answers or be extroverted or do everything perfectly. Caring is the ongoing action of bringing our presence to people's lives, investing in relationship, and being with them and for them as they journey toward the One who loves them. In Christ's love, we show up because we care about *people Jesus died for*, not because we have a quota to fill. We care because we want people to experience the goodness of God! We know that God's love is better than life.[12] But the first way many people will experience that goodness is by experiencing one of God's children loving them. Evangelism is simply a former orphan telling other orphans about how they can be adopted by our good Father.

The Gospel Is a Feast

I love Pappadeaux Seafood Kitchen. I order the same food every time I visit because it's epic! When I walk in, a thousand mouthwatering scents reach my nose and remind my taste buds of the deliciousness I am about to experience. I don't even need to look at the menu because I am going to order Mississippi Catfish Opelousas, which is covered in oysters, shrimp, jumbo lump crab, and lemon garlic butter sauce, with dirty rice. I want everyone to try it because it's amazing!

Through the life, death, and resurrection of Jesus, you and I get to experience the never-ending, abundant gospel feast. We've tasted the goodness of Jesus, the Bread of Life, and the living waters of mercy. As we go through our days, a thousand experiences of grace awaken our hearts and souls to the God who loves us and has thrown the doors of his Kingdom open wide to welcome us in.

When you're lit up with love, you are inviting other orphans to our Father's house to sit at his immense table of grace, where they can find drink to quench their thirst, food to satisfy their hunger, and forgiveness that atones for their sin. Why wouldn't we want other people to join us at this overflowing table? Why wouldn't we want them to step in, blinking from the darkness, to experience the colors and beauty and joy of living in the light? As everyday missionaries, we have the privilege of leading people—wisely, gently, and graciously—to the table of Christ, where grace is freely given without limit. We get to carry a torch into their cold darkness and help them move toward the bright Son. The world is dark. Go light it up with love.

Holy Habits

- *When you're lit up with love, you understand that belonging often precedes believing.*

- *When you're lit up with love, you understand that your own discipleship and transformation are priorities.*

- *When you're lit up with love, you know that before you talk to people about Jesus, you must talk to Jesus about people.*

- *When you're lit up with love, you are burdened to see the lost found, and that holy burden moves you to prayer.*

- *When you're lit up with love, you are inviting other orphans to our Father's house to sit at his immense table of grace, where they can find drink to quench their thirst, food to satisfy their hunger, and forgiveness that atones for their sin.*

Reflection Questions

1. What are some creative ways you can be available to share the gospel in your daily life?

2. How can you intentionally invite lost people into belonging through your missional presence?

3. Why is your personal discipleship important for evangelism?

4. What ways of sharing your faith feel most natural to you?

5. Which of the Scriptures referenced in this chapter motivate you to reach lost people? Consider incorporating one or more into a regular rhythm of prayer.

PRAYER

Lord Jesus,

Open my eyes so that I might see the harvest.

Holy Spirit,

Anoint me to embody the gospel

and share it with power and love.

Father,

Lead me to your lost children.

Amen.

Acknowledgments

To my wife, Vicki—you are my best friend and partner in the gospel! Anything I do, you do, because we are one. Thank you for loving me.

To my daughter, Presley—in 2018, walking in the streets of Copenhagen, Denmark, you challenged me to write books for God's glory. This is my fifth book since that talk!

Thank you, Jeremiah—your faith and disciplined life make me want to be a better man. Thank you, Son. Your encouragement strengthens me.

Caitlyn Carlson and NavPress—it's an honor to change the world with you. Thank you for believing in me!

To my agent, Alexander Field—you are the best! Thank you.

Lastly, thank you, Transformation Church—you are lit up with love! You are Good-News people in a gospel-starved world! It's a pleasure to serve with you in this adventure!

Notes

CHAPTER 0 | WHERE ARE YOU GOING?

1. 1 Corinthians 15:54, csb.
2. Revelation 7:9.
3. Revelation 1:5-6.
4. Ephesians 5:8-9.

CHAPTER 1 | LET'S TALK ABOUT GOOD NEWS

1. Genesis 50:20.
2. John 16:33, csb.
3. Genesis 50:20; Romans 8:28-29.
4. Michael J. Gorman, *Becoming the Gospel: Paul, Participation, and Mission* (Grand Rapids: Eerdmans, 2015), 24.
5. Colossians 1:19-20.
6. Psalm 63:3-5.
7. 1 John 4:16.
8. Luke 7:34.
9. Colossians 2:12-15.
10. Kenneth Boa, *Conformed to His Image: Biblical, Practical Approaches to Spiritual Formation*, rev. ed. (Grand Rapids: Zondervan Academic, 2020), 414.
11. 2 Peter 3:9, csb.
12. 1 Corinthians 3:6-9.
13. Luke 4:16-18.
14. Matthew 28:18-20.

15. Dallas Willard, "Rethinking Evangelism," Dallas Willard Ministries, accessed July 27, 2023, https://dwillard.org/articles/rethinking -evangelism. Originally published in *Cutting Edge* (Winter 2001).
16. Matthew 13:45-46.

CHAPTER 2 | WHAT IS THE GOOD NEWS?

1. 2 Corinthians 5:14-15.
2. Isaiah 42:6-7.
3. 1 John 4:8.
4. John 1:4-5.
5. Hebrews 1:3, csb.
6. John 1:14; Philippians 2:6-11; 1 Timothy 2:5-6.
7. Matthew 5:44-45; Romans 12:20.
8. John 14:6.
9. John 8:58.
10. John 1:5.
11. John 8:12.
12. Acts 2:23-24.
13. Exodus 19:5-6.
14. John 5:39.
15. Galatians 3:8, 14, 26-29.
16. Hebrews 12:1-2.
17. 1 Timothy 2:5-6.
18. In the Old Testament, the Hebrew term *son* (*bēn*) is sometimes used to refer to the men and women in the nation of Israel. *Son* was a term of belovedness. Because Jesus is the eternal Son of God, through faith in Jesus, men and women share in his sonship. See Exodus 4:22-23; Hosea 11:1; Ephesians 1:3-7.
19. 2 Peter 1:4.
20. Mark 1:15; Luke 4:16-21.
21. John 17:18.
22. In my book *God, Do You Hear Me?: Discover the Prayer God Always Answers* (Nashville: B&H, 2021), I share in detail about the Kingdom of God.
23. Colossians 1:13-14; 1 Peter 2:9.
24. Matthew 22:37-39; 28:18-20; 2 Corinthians 5:18-20; Galatians 2:20.
25. John 3:16-19.

26. 1 Corinthians 15:35-58; Revelation 5:9; 21:3-4. A common question that you will get is this: "What about those who have never heard of Jesus? How can they be judged for rejecting a message and person they've never heard of?" I believe that no such person will exist because if people respond in faith to the *Light of Creation* and the *Light of Consciousness*, the triune God will give them the *Light of Christ*, leading to salvation. I regularly meet former Muslims who now follow Jesus because Jesus appeared to them in a dream. God is good and merciful. He will not leave himself without a witness.

    Light of Creation: "His invisible attributes, that is, his eternal power and divine nature, have been clearly seen since the creation of the world, being understood through what he has made. As a result, people are without excuse" (Romans 1:20, CSB).

    Light of Consciousness: "When Gentiles, who do not by nature have the law, do what the law demands, they are a law to themselves even though they do not have the law. They show that the work of the law is written on their hearts. Their consciences confirm this. Their competing thoughts either accuse or even excuse them" (Romans 2:14-15, CSB).

    Light of Christ: "There is salvation in no one else, for there is no other name under heaven given to people by which we must be saved" (Acts 4:12, CSB).

27. Philippians 3:7-8.
28. E. Stanley Jones, *The Christ of the Indian Road* (New York: Abingdon Press, 1925), 12.
29. Romans 10:15.

CHAPTER 3 | STARVED FOR HOPE

1. J. R. R. Tolkien, *The Two Towers: Being the Second Part of The Lord of the Rings*, 2nd ed. (Boston: Houghton Mifflin, 1982), 308.
2. The world (1 John 2:15-17), the flesh or sin nature (1 Peter 2:11), and the devil (1 Peter 5:8).
3. Ephesians 5:31-32.
4. Romans 15:13, CSB.
5. Matthew 7:24-25.
6. 1 Peter 1:3, CSB.
7. 1 Corinthians 3:6-9.

CHAPTER 4 | STARVED FOR REST

1. Matthew 11:28-30.
2. For a list of places in the Scriptures these names for God are used, see "The Names of God in the Old Testament," Blue Letter Bible, accessed August 7, 2024, https://www.blueletterbible.org/study/misc/name_god.cfm.
3. Romans 8:1.
4. John 1:29; 10:14-18, 27-30.
5. Isaiah 53:6.
6. Romans 8:31-39.
7. 1 Peter 2:24-25.
8. Luke 15:3-7.
9. John 10:14-16.
10. Colossians 3:3-4.
11. John 10:9.
12. Hebrews 4:9.
13. John 10:10.

CHAPTER 5 | STARVED FOR HEALING

1. 2 Corinthians 5:17.
2. John 1:16.
3. Ephesians 2:8-9.
4. Ephesians 2:1-4.
5. Romans 5:8.
6. Isaiah 53:4-6.
7. 1 Corinthians 1:30-31.
8. Ephesians 1:3-14.
9. John 1:16, CSB.
10. John 10:28; Romans 8:35-39; 1 Corinthians 6:11; Hebrews 10:14.
11. Romans 6:6-11.
12. Exodus 3:19.
13. Exodus 12:7-14.
14. Exodus 12:31-32, NIV.
15. Ephesians 1:6-7.
16. Romans 5:8-11.

17. Ephesians 1:5.
18. The statement "There is no saint without a past, no sinner without a future" is accredited to Saint Augustine.
19. 2 Corinthians 5:18-20.
20. John 15:13-14.
21. Matthew 5:8; 2 Corinthians 5:18-20.
22. Romans 3:22; 2 Corinthians 5:21; Ephesians 1:4.
23. Romans 8:1.
24. 1 Corinthians 1:30.
25. Romans 5:8-9.
26. Galatians 5:22-24.
27. Romans 8:28-30.
28. Romans 2:4.
29. Ephesians 2:9-10.
30. Galatians 5:22-23.
31. Romans 6:1-14; Galatians 2:20; Ephesians 3:14-21; Colossians 1:27.

CHAPTER 6 | STARVED FOR NEW LIFE

1. John 1:12-13.
2. Romans 6:3-6.
3. 1 Peter 1:18.
4. Romans 5:19-21.
5. Romans 3:23-24.
6. John 11:25.
7. 1 Peter 2:9.
8. 1 Peter 1:7-8; 3:18.
9. Titus 2:14, NIV.
10. Matthew 5:16.
11. Matthew 6:10.
12. Galatians 5:22-23.
13. Galatians 2:20; Ephesians 1:15-23.
14. Fred Sanders, *Wesley on the Christian Life: The Heart Renewed in Love* (Wheaton, IL: Crossway, 2013), 33.
15. Sanders, *Wesley on the Christian Life*, 98–99.
16. Sanders, *Wesley on the Christian Life*, 99.

CHAPTER 7 | EVERYDAY MISSIONARIES

1. Matthew 28:18-20.
2. 2 Corinthians 5:20.
3. Luke 19:10; Philippians 2:5-11.
4. 2 Corinthians 5:14-15.
5. 2 Corinthians 4:5-6.
6. 1 Corinthians 2:2, CSB.
7. Galatians 5:16, 22-24.
8. Acts 11:20, CSB.
9. Acts 17.
10. Acts 17:16-34; 1 Corinthians 9:22-23.

CHAPTER 8 | EVERYTHING THAT HINDERS

1. Acts 7:51.
2. Acts 17:32-34.
3. Aaron Earls, "Christians Don't Share Faith with Unchurched Friends," Lifeway Research, September 9, 2021, https://research .lifeway.com/2021/09/09/christians-dont-share-faith-with -unchurched-friends.
4. Kenneth Boa, *Conformed to His Image: Biblical, Practical Approaches to Spiritual Formation*, rev. ed. (Grand Rapids: Zondervan Academic, 2020), 422–29. I've followed Boa's basic framework here but replaced his Barrier of Isolation with the Barrier of Shame.
5. John 15:5-8.
6. 1 Corinthians 15:10.
7. 1 Corinthians 10:32.
8. 1 John 4:18.
9. Boa, *Conformed to His Image*, 423.
10. 1 Corinthians 12:3, CSB.
11. John 12:32; 2 Peter 3:9.
12. Acts 1:8.
13. 2 Timothy 1:7.
14. 1 Peter 3:15.
15. 2 Timothy 2:15. Here are some apologetics resources: Timothy Keller, *The Reason for God: Belief in an Age of Skepticism*; Norman L. Geisler and Frank Turek, *I Don't Have Enough Faith to Be an Atheist*; Dan

Kimball, *How (Not) to Read the Bible: Making Sense of the Anti-Women, Anti-Science, Pro-Violence, Pro-Slavery and Other Crazy Sounding Parts of Scripture.*

16. 1 Peter 3:15-16.

17. Revelation 2:4.

18. Mark 4:19, CSB.

19. See derwinlgray.com/churchkit for our church implementation kit, which includes spiritual-discipline prompts and more.

20. Matthew 28:18-20; Ephesians 4:12-16.

21. 1 John 5:11-13.

22. Every human being, regardless of who they are or what they've done, is worthy of dignity, honor, and respect. As a follower of Jesus, I can love you without affirming certain behaviors. Being straight does not save us. Being LGBTQ+ does not save us. Jesus saves us by grace alone. And when Jesus saves us by grace, he transforms us by giving us new hearts with new desires. This does not mean that certain temptations or feelings go away. It means that as we obey Jesus, our lives become more congruent with his Kingdom's ethics.

23. Matthew 5:4.

24. Caroline Dowd-Higgins, "Being Busy Is Nothing to Brag About," *Chicago Tribune*, updated May 13, 2019, https://www.chicagotribune.com/2018/02/08/being-busy-is-nothing-to-brag-about.

25. 1 John 4:18.

CHAPTER 9 | REMOVE EVERY OBSTACLE

1. Tim Keller, "The Supremacy of Christ and the Gospel in a Postmodern World," DesiringGod.org, September 30, 2006, https://www.desiringgod.org/messages/the-supremacy-of-christ-and-the-gospel-in-a-postmodern-world.

2. Romans 3:10-11.

3. Barna Group, "What Does It Mean to Be Spiritually Open?" June 21, 2023, https://www.barna.com/research/spiritual-openness.

4. Acts 11:25-26.

5. Acts 17:22-23.

6. As quoted in John R. W. Stott, *The Message of Acts: The Spirit, the Church and the World* (Leicester, England: InterVarsity Press, 1990), 277.

7. Matthew 27:37.

8. John 8:58.

9. Acts 17:6-8, CSB.

10. N. T. Wright and Michael F. Bird, *The New Testament in Its World: An Introduction to the History, Literature, and Theology of the First Christians* (Grand Rapids: Zondervan Academic, 2019), 814–15.

11. 1 Corinthians 10:20.

12. John 10:10.

13. John 14:6, NIV.

14. Acts 4:12.

15. N. T. Wright, *Paul: A Biography* (New York: HarperOne, 2018), 11.

16. These projections are based on a 2022 study by Gordon-Conwell Theological Seminary's Center for the Study of Global Christianity. For a snapshot of the report, see "Status of World Christianity, 2024, in the Context of 1900–2050," https://www.gordonconwell.edu /center-for-global-christianity/resources/status-of-global-christianity.

17. Jeremiah 29:7, NIV.

18. Acts 10:34-35, ESV.

19. William Barclay, *The Letters to the Galatians and Ephesians*, The New Daily Study Bible, rev. ed. (Louisville, KY: Westminster John Knox Press, 2002), 130.

20. See "Birchot HaShachar," Hebrew for Christians, accessed August 12, 2024, https://www.hebrew4christians.com/Blessings/Synagogue _Blessings/Birchot_HaShachar/birchot_hashachar.html. Here is a traditional rendering of a line from morning blessings that appear in the siddur (a Jewish prayer book). Contemporary renderings put this in the context of gratefulness for Jewish identity rather than as an indictment on non-Jews, women, and slaves.

21. Acts 10:28, NIV.

22. See my book *How to Heal Our Racial Divide: What the Bible Says, and the First Christians Knew, about Racial Reconciliation* (Carol Stream, IL: Tyndale Momentum, 2022).

23. Galatians 3:27-29; Ephesians 2:14-22; Colossians 3:11.

24. 2 Corinthians 5:14-21.

25. Acts 17:16.

26. Acts 17:18-33.

27. Galatians 3:8-29.
28. 1 John 4:20.
29. Galatians 3:24-29.
30. Acts 17:22-23.
31. Acts 17:22-29.
32. Stott, *Message of Acts*, 285–87.
33. Stott, *Message of Acts*, 290.
34. Acts 17:30-31.
35. 2 Peter 3:9.
36. Acts 17:34, csb.

CHAPTER 10 | OPEN YOUR EYES
1. Luke 24:13-39; John 5:39-40.
2. John 15:5.
3. Romans 2:12-15.
4. 2 Corinthians 2:15-16.
5. Mark 12:31.
6. 1 Corinthians 13:1-3.
7. Acts 2:14-38.
8. Acts 8:26-40.
9. 1 Thessalonians 2:8.
10. Luke 10:25-37.
11. 2 Timothy 3:16, niv.
12. Psalm 63:3.